PRACTICAL WISDOM FOR PASTORS

Words of Encouragement and Counsel
for a Lifetime of Ministry

D0109205

CURTIS C. THOMAS

CROSSWAY BOOKS

A PUBLISHING MINISTRY OF
GOOD NEWS PUBLISHERS
WHEATON, ILLINOIS

Library of Congress Cataloging-in-Publication Data
Thomas, Curtis C., 1937-
    Practical wisdom for pastors : words of encouragement and counsel for
a lifetime of ministry / Curtis C. Thomas.
        p.   cm.
    Includes bibliographical references.
    ISBN 13: 978-1-58134-252-9
    ISBN 10: 1-58134-252-7 (alk. paper)
    1. Clergy—Office. 2. Encouragement—Religious aspects—Christianity.
I. Title.
BV660.3.T47   2001
253—dc21   00-011653

BP		17	16	15	14	13	12	11	10	09	08	07	06
18	17	16	15	14	13	12	11	10	9	8	7	6	5	4

This book is dedicated to four individuals whom God has graciously and sovereignly brought into my life.

To my three sons
Alan Christian, wise and gentle;
Keith Douglas, fiercely dedicated; and
Robert Scott, hardworking and generous.
They have made me thankful and have taught me how to live in so many ways.

And to
J. Todd Murray, young and extremely gifted, my friend and former co-pastor, who in sixteen years of ministry has grown immensely and has embodied what it means to shepherd both his family and a growing flock of God's sheep.

NOTE:

Throughout this material the titles *pastor, elder, shepherd, minister, bishop,* and *overseer* will be used synonymously. The Scriptures use these titles for the same office and work (see 1 Tim. 3:1-7; 4:6; 5:17-20; Titus 1:5-9; 1 Pet. 5:1-4; Acts 20:28); so they will be used interchangeably here.

If you find portions of this material helpful and wish to use it for the benefit of others, please feel free to do so. I would ask that the publisher be contacted first when excerpts exceed 500 words.

TABLE OF CONTENTS

Section Four: Messages

Section Five: Church Life

Acknowledgments

Few, if any, books are the product of one person. This work is no exception. Through the years I have become tremendously indebted to the writings and ministries of many outstanding servants of the Lord who have helped me by their careful exegesis and sound motivation. In addition, the present work has been impacted by the encouragements, reviews, comments, helpful suggestions, and corrections by a number of men and women: Dr. Jay Adams, Kenny Allison, Dr. John Armstrong, Tom Arnold, Dr. Frank Barker, John Blanchard, Charles Borth, Bill Etter, Richard Fulenwider, Larry and Dolores Fisher, Theron Howard, Carl Hunt, Dr. Rick Houk, Phil Johnson, Dr. D. James Kennedy, Dr. Steve Lawson, Dr. John MacArthur, Pastor Carter Mills, Dr. Albert Mohler, Jr., Dr. David Powlison, Gerry Puls, Pastor Lance Quinn, Dennis Rainey, Pastor Tim Reed, Pastor Adrian Rogers, Neil Shaver, George Shipp, Bill Simmons, Dr. Jack Somers, Calvin Squires, and Joe and Kathy Walker. I acknowledge their generous assistance and encouragement. Each person has contributed in various ways, though all shortcomings in the final product are my responsibility.

A special word of thanks goes to Ted Griffin, Managing Editor of Crossway Books, for his very thorough assistance and encouragement.

I am further indebted to John Blanchard for his excellent trilogy—*Gathered Gold, More Gathered Gold,* and *Sifted Silver,* three books that are filled with excellent material. Many of the quotations at the beginning of these articles have been gleaned from these books. Blanchard's works are treasures. Thank you, John, for your work.

Finally, I want to express my love and appreciation for my wife, Betty, who has for more than forty years been my most insightful and faithful supporter. Once again, through this work, she has painstakingly edited, corrected, questioned, challenged, and encouraged me. Her many hours of patient work continue to demonstrate what a wonderful helpmate God has given me.

FOREWORD

Curtis Thomas has culled a wealth of practical insights from a lifetime of fruitful ministry, and he has distilled it in a book that will be a rich source of help and encouragement for pastors and church leaders everywhere. Curtis Thomas writes with the heart of a pastor who is devoted to his Lord. His deep love for the Word of God is evident throughout. And his commitment to biblical ministry sets the tone for the book.

I wish this book had been available when I began in ministry more than thirty-five years ago. It covers virtually all the vital aspects of the pastor's work that cannot adequately be learned in a classroom context. As I read, I found my own enthusiasm for pastoral ministry invigorated; and even as a veteran pastor, I found much I could benefit from in Curtis Thomas's catalog of practical wisdom. He has given pastors everywhere an invaluable resource.

Certain pitfalls seem common to most young pastors. I often hear young pastors wonder aloud why there is no book that deals with such things. Now there is, and it should be required reading not only for young men beginning their ministries, but for anyone who wants to be more effective in any role of church leadership.

Years ago, near the outset of his ministry, Curtis Thomas coauthored a little booklet called *The Five Points of Calvinism* that has helped untold numbers come to grips with what Scripture teaches about the doctrine of God's sovereignty in salvation. That book is still in print and selling briskly. Now, having retired from full-time pastoral work, Pastor Thomas has given us another work of equal or even greater import. My prayer is that it will also find a vast readership, and that it will be used of God to edify and equip church leaders for many generations to come.

John MacArthur

INTRODUCTION

This book is about material that I wish had been available to me before I was asked to stand before a small congregation and preach my first sermon many years ago. Most of the discussions in this book were relevant then, and are still relevant today—perhaps more so today since the temptations are now more open and inviting, and the problems pastors now face can be much more involved due to the complexities of modern culture.

It has now been forty-five years since my first message before that small, independent Baptist church in Arkansas. Since then I have been privileged to serve as a lay pastor for a number of years, and then later in a full-time ministry. During those days my ministry took the form of a sole pastor in a small congregation, then as a co-pastor of a larger, growing congregation, and during the last fourteen years serving as the executive pastor in a still larger congregation with multiple pastors.

During those years I made many mistakes—both minor and significant ones. A pastor can face many traps. I know because I stumbled into a number of them. They hurt, especially when your mistakes become public. I have also painfully watched some of my coworkers become entrapped in situations that adversely affected them and their ministries. Some of our mistakes seem to bear few consequences, while others seriously affect not only us, but our families and our congregations as well.

Years ago a young pastor was seldom thrust onto a congregation without first having served as an understudy to a more senior pastor, so he could learn from the wisdom of his elder. But today it seems as if a seminary degree is all that is required to become a "senior" pastor. Often when that occurs, the church is led by a young man who has had little or no experience with the real world of church life. When problems come flooding in, the young pastor suffers. At times he falls into everyday, common pitfalls that leave him dazed, disillusioned, and often very lonely. At other times he may try things that a more experienced pastor realizes simply will not work. He becomes frustrated. Many times his first church becomes his last church. Or else he continues with deep hurts and disappointments while his family suffers, the church is set back, and the cause of Christ is damaged.

Had he known beforehand some of the experiences he must face and some of the pitfalls to avoid, perhaps his life and his church would have taken a different path. The old saying that an ounce of prevention is worth a pound of cure is certainly appropriate regarding the ministry. The ministry is a public platform. Mistakes in the ministry affect many people simply due to the public nature of the work. In this arena, wisdom is to be truly prized.

The book of Proverbs contains short, pithy words of wisdom. I have always especially appreciated that portion of God's inspired Word because it gets to the point and often repeats it to help us get the message. Getting to the point without extra words has been my objective in these short sections. Perhaps these thoughts, though brief, could be mulled over privately or could even spark conversations in which these matters are explored in more depth than I have covered here.

To facilitate deeper investigation into many of the areas covered, after each of the ten major sections I have included biblical references and a bibliography of printed material at the end of the book. In addition, toward the end of the book you will find two very helpful appendices. The first one is an article that was printed in *The Journal of Biblical Counseling* and was titled "Pastor's Self-Evaluation Questionnaire," by Dr. Tim Keller and Dr. David Powlison. This excellent work will help the pastor test his humility, love, integrity, spirituality, nurture, communication, and leadership.

The second article was printed in *RTS Ministry* (now being published as *RTS REFORMED Quarterly*) and was titled "What Should a Sermon Do?" It was written by Dr. William Hogan. In this work Dr. Hogan demonstrates that a sermon should make the truth of Scripture crystal-clear, help the listener feel the claim of the biblical text, press that claim upon the hearer's will, and ultimately lead the listener to an encounter with the God of truth. For preaching pastors, this can hardly be stated more clearly.

The pastor must be an expositor and a counselor and must minister to the needs of his congregation. There is an outstanding trilogy that covers in depth these three areas. The book you have in your hand merely scratches the surface, but the following volumes cover the topics in detail. Purchase these three volumes and live with them, and your pastorate will take on new depth: John MacArthur, Jr. and The Master's Seminary Faculty, *Rediscovering Expository Preaching*, Word, 1992; John MacArthur, Jr., Wayne Mack, and The Master's College Faculty, *Introduction to Biblical Counseling*, Word, 1994; John MacArthur, Jr. and The Master's Seminary Faculty, *Rediscovering Pastoral Ministry*, Word, 1995.

Erwin Lutzer, senior pastor of Moody Church, Chicago, recently revised and expanded his *Pastor to Pastor*, an insightful book on how the pastor can handle difficult situations. In it he covers topics such as the call to the ministry, problem people, church splits, burnout, public invitations, and fallen pastors. His experience, maturity, biblical insight, and interesting anecdotes will provide both the young and mature pastor with valuable help. Though the number of topics he covers is limited, his book should be read carefully. While *Practical Wisdom for Pastors* covers a broader range of subjects, Lutzer's work provides more in-depth treatment. Secure a copy, and heed his wise advice.

As pastors, we serve as leaders, shepherds, fathers, and sometimes as mothers to our congregations. Serving as examples, we should be aware of the mistakes that can lie ahead and skillfully avoid them as we lead our congregations in wise and godly living. Some seminaries do a creditable job of preparing young men for the challenges ahead, while others involve their students primarily in the world of academics. In such cases practical counsel and training is needed.

Though many of these brief articles deal with daily problems encountered in the ministry, I want to emphasize the satisfaction and joy pastors have as they see God marvelously change people for eternity. To see souls converted, believers grow in grace and knowledge, lives put back together, and marriages saved and strengthened makes other problems pale in comparison. For most of us the ministry is not only a profession but a true labor of love.

These thoughts are not written from the perspective of one who has had it all together or who has always acted wisely, but as a fellow traveler who has made his share of mistakes and who has at times acted very unwisely. I wish I could tell you that I have learned all of the lessons about which I write. But I cannot. Like the apostle Paul, much of what I hate, I do, and much of what I want to do, I do not. Though having had a long ministry, I still want to grow in all of these critical areas, and I assure you that I have not yet arrived where I want to be. However, should God be pleased to use these brief thoughts to help you in your role as a godly leader, may He be praised.

Curtis Thomas

PERSONAL

LIFE

Our Call

HOW CAN WE KNOW IT IS AUTHENTIC?

Whatever "call" a man may pretend to have, if he has not been called
to holiness, he certainly has not been called to the ministry.
—CHARLES H. SPURGEON

The call to the ministry has been described in many ways. Some say they have received a direct revelation from God telling them audibly that He has chosen them for their special work. Others describe their call as coming to them in a dream or some mystical experience. Another will say God actually appeared to him in a vision to call him into the ministry. Some preachers say their call was an overwhelming compulsion to become a pastor, or the feeling that they were a misfit in every other occupation and thereby could not find happiness until they "surrendered to the ministry."

Thus one can see how the general public would be very confused by what has been designated "the call to the ministry."

Let's look for a moment at the Scriptures. First Timothy 3:1 says that the elder (pastor) must desire or reach out for the office. First Timothy 5:22 says that we must "not be hasty in the laying on of hands," meaning that we should be careful about whom we recognize as candidates for the ministry. First Timothy 3:1-7, Titus 1:5-9, and 1 Peter 5:1-4 teach us that to fill the office, the person must be qualified by certain moral characteristics. In the 1 Peter passage the person must be an example to the flock. First Timothy 4:9-16 tells us that the pastor's "life and doctrine" must be sound. That would require that the church make an assessment of the men who reach out for the office. And 1 Timothy 5:17-21 gives us instructions on to how to correct an elder who sins and, by implication, does not measure up to the office.

So, to summarize: The biblical concept of a "call to the ministry" does not include a vision, special revelation, or mystical experience.

Rather, it involves factors such as: (1) Does the man reach out for the work? (2) Is he qualified biblically? (3) Does he possess the gifts necessary to fulfill the functions? (4) Do the elders and the church think he is gifted and morally qualified? (5) Are his life and doctrine sound? (6) Will he live as an example before the flock?

It is true that in the Old Testament and in the first century of Christianity, God did intervene directly and call men to ministry. But today His revelation has been completed by the New Testament, and it is our reliable guide. Therefore, a local church should be able to take God's Word and help the candidate assess whether or not he has been called to the gospel ministry.

PERSONAL DEVOTIONAL LIFE
PASTORAL DUTIES MUST NOT CROWD IT OUT

Very early in the morning, while it was still dark, Jesus got up, left the house and went off to a solitary place, where he prayed.
—MARK 1:35

After entering the ministry, I found it difficult to cultivate a personal devotional life. That may surprise you, but the problem was manifold. Among the reasons were late-night meetings and counseling times, early-morning staff and committee meetings, and the constant demand to prepare notes, lessons, sermons, and the like. In addition, there were so many needs in the congregation about which I needed to pray that they took up most of my own prayer time. In fact, part of the blessings I looked forward to in retirement was the regular and extended opportunity to feed my own soul.

It came as a surprise to me that one of the problems I faced in the ministry was that when I opened the Scriptures I found it extremely difficult to forget the need to determine the background, outline the passage, divide it into an appropriate package for delivery, and think of ways to get this particular truth across to others. It became very difficult for me to just sit down with the Scriptures and let them speak to me, alone. Also my prayers, which certainly were needed for my own personal needs, would often drift off into the pressing needs of our church body.

That makes it tough on one's personal devotional times. Perhaps some can discipline their minds better, but I found it difficult. I don't really think I was trying to escape my own responsibilities. Rather, after being in the ministry for a period of time, we know about so many hurting people in the congregation, so many people who need to change their actions, attitudes, or thinking, and so many who need to be involved in specific service opportunities that they often take first priority in our minds. With the Scriptures in hand, we see many verses that address their particular situation, and thus our own personal devotional time becomes intercessory work.

Our own personal devotional time becomes intercessory work.

I am not sure I have a good solution. Perhaps getting away regularly, taking the first day or two to help cleanse your mind of the urgent problems, and then a day or two just between you and the Lord, would be one way. Reading and praying with our wives on a regular basis is helpful also. Each pastor will have a different circumstance, and so how each one solves this dilemma will be different. But it does deserve constant attention.

It would be a great tragedy to see our members growing in service and godliness, while our own souls are starving for personal fellowship with our Lord!

PRAYER

OUR LIFEBLOOD AND REAL POWER

He that is more frequent in his pulpit to his people than he is in his closet for his people is but a sorry watchman.   —John Owen

Sure, we are involved in prayer all the time. We pray before and after each sermon. We pray at the church prayer meetings. We are often the one called on to open meetings with prayer. We wouldn't think of eating a meal without at least someone offering thanksgiving. When we visit people at the hospital, we pray for them. At secular events or sporting events, we are often called on to offer the opening prayer.

In our public life we are men of prayer. But what about in our private lives? Are we men of prayer then? That's the acid test. The public occasions can be mere performance. The private times demonstrate whether we are men of spiritual integrity.

Prayer is an acknowledgment that we are needy individuals. It also demonstrates to us our personal relationship with our Lord. And it reflects our genuine love and concern for our flock as we labor in prayer for their spiritual good.

Prayer is an acknowledgment that we are needy individuals. It also demonstrates to us our personal relationship with our Lord.

As a young pastor I once asked an aging pastor about his readily apparent spiritual life. He explained to me that he arose at 4:00 every morning to begin his two-hour daily, private prayer life. He spent the first hour each day acknowledging the Lord's wonderful attributes and His goodness. Then he moved into requests for the remaining hour. He said that those two hours were the most important of his daily functions.

There was no doubt that this man's personal godliness came as a direct result of his daily communion with the Lord. Just as Spurgeon spoke of John Bunyan when he said that if you "pricked him, his blood flowed Bibline," so if you were to prick that faithful, aged pastor, he would flow grace, gentleness, and holiness.

Do we want deep spiritual lifeblood and power? It starts with a personal relationship with our God. We know Him through His eternal Word, but we communicate with Him through prayer.

We can fake a spiritual life by public prayer, but the One who knows us best cannot be fooled. God can give us real power in our ministry, or He can withhold His grace as we fail to develop that deeply needed personal relationship with Him.

ACCOUNTABILITY PARTNERS

WE ALL NEED ONE OR MORE HONEST FRIENDS

A friend loves at all times, and a brother is born for adversity.
—PROVERBS 17:17

Nothing is more stimulating than friends who speak the truth in love.
—OS GUINNESS

It is the best and truest friend who honestly tells us the truth about ourselves even when he knows we shall not like it. False friends are the ones who hide such truth from us and do so in order to remain in our favour. —R. C. H. LENSKI

It is a luxury to have people with whom we can let our hair down and just be ourselves. Pastors especially need that sort of relationship because as public figures we are always on display and open to close scrutiny. But as human beings we also sin, have weaknesses, suffer from fears, have hang-ups, and live with emotions, both good and bad.

Obviously, pastors' wives must be their number one resource to fill the need for friendship. Our relationship with our wives must be open and honest. She can be our faithful critic and comforter. She can help us analyze, plan, correct, implement, and react properly. Apart from Christ and our salvation, she is God's greatest gift to us.

But it is also helpful and necessary to have other close (male) friends who will be painfully honest with us without the emotional involvement of our wives. These men can call us to account, tell us when we are thinking incorrectly or reacting emotionally, ask the hard questions, not let us slide by or dodge an issue, and stand by us when they think we are right. These men can also honestly assess our leadership, our messages, and our shepherding. We need their help in all of these areas.

Who should they be? Preferably one or two should come from our own congregation and perhaps one or two from another ministry or geographical setting. By selecting men from those two areas, we gain the advantage of having friendly critics within the sphere of our ministry and also those who have no personal involvement in our ministry and thus can provide a bit more objectivity.

It does no good to have such accountability partners if we do not take the time to be with them and do not open up before them. They are not little gods and cannot read our minds, and they do not always know how to read between the lines.

There will definitely be things that these men should keep in strict confidence, but in other areas they must be free to talk with our wives or elders or associates. Without trying to be specific in this area with examples, there may be those times when our accountability partners cannot be bound to total confidentiality since they may judge that the situation calls for us to make a public apology or undergo some form of public correction.

True friends are wonderful gifts from God. Proverbs 18:24 says they will stick "closer than a brother." And their wounds are definitely better for us than the kisses of our enemies (Prov. 27:6).

ADMITTING MISTAKES
IT IS BEST TO ADMIT THEM AND MOVE ON

He that is down needs fear no fall; he that is low, no pride. He that is humble ever shall have God to be his guide.   —JOHN BUNYAN

Let's admit it. Sometimes we are wrong. At times we say things that we learn later are incorrect. There are times when our judgment is poor. At times our reactions will be purely emotional and improper. And worst of all, our pride wells up inside us, and we just don't like to speak the three hardest words in the English language: "I was wrong."

But there can be no better way to lead a group of people than to admit our human weaknesses. Mistakes are part of the human predicament. As we continue to study, there will be times when we will change our minds on points of theology or the way we have interpreted a passage. When we do, we must not only correct our personal position but let our congregation know also.

The point is, at times we are going to be wrong, and we need to be humble enough to admit it, make the correcton, and move on.

I know of a pastor who began as an Arminian. Over the years he has become an outspoken Calvinist. This is clear to everyone. Yet he maintains that his understanding of the Scriptures has always been Calvinistic. He needs to acknowledge to the congregation that his study over the years has led him to a new conclusion, that his theology was defective, and that by the grace of God he now has a better grasp of the Scriptures. Such is not a weakness but a strength. Those who will not learn should not teach.

I also remember hearing a true story about a man who was committed to the position that a believer could fall from grace. He began a series defending that position. In one of his sermons he was preaching through John 10. Right in the middle of delivering his sermon his eyes were opened to what Jesus was saying. He stopped his sermon and explained to his congregation that he now saw clearly the opposite position taught in this passage. He finished the sermon proclaiming the preservation of the believer. That is an outstanding example of a man who was willing to admit his error immediately once the truth was made clear before his eyes.

We will not only be wrong on theological positions, but in implementing certain programs in our church, or in the shepherding of certain members, or in choosing message topics. The point is, at times we are going to be wrong, and we need to be humble enough to admit it, make the correction, and move on.

Our members will usually be very forgiving and ready to support us in our new direction, providing we teach them enough to show them the error of our ways and the correctness of our new approach. Members appreciate leaders who will acknowledge their humanness and those who are willing to ask to be forgiven.

OUR FINANCIAL REPUTATIONS
IMPROPER STEWARDSHIP CAN DESTROY OUR MINISTRY

Let no debt remain outstanding. —ROMANS 13:8

Years ago a credit company informed me that insurance salesmen and pastors were the nation's worst credit risks. Another company said that professions beginning with the letter *p* were bad risks: preacher, painter, policeman, politician. Whether or not such reports are true, at least they contain some bad publicity for the ministry. We constantly live in a fishbowl. And the way we handle our financial affairs will certainly come to light.

Let's face it, the ministry generally is not a lucrative occupation. Most pastors have to struggle financially to make ends meet. The story has been told that a deacon once remarked that pastors should be poor and humble, and if the Lord would keep them humble, the deacons would see to it that their pastors were kept poor. And it seems that sometimes such is the case. Pastors are viewed by those who do not really know the burdens they carry as having easy jobs with flexible hours, only really working forty-five minutes a week on Sundays. You and I know better. Yet often the pay structure is loosely based on that perspective. And that increases the financial burden on the ministry.

> We constantly live in a fishbowl.
> And the way we handle our financial affairs
> will certainly come to light.

But that goes with the territory, at least until the deacons, the church leadership, and the members are duly educated as to the duties of the job when well done. They need to know that it is an advantage to the church when she gives double honor to her faithful pastors. The church I was privileged to serve before retirement recognized the pastoral needs and did a wonderful job of providing for all of us. The salaries and full benefits package were very adequate.

Regardless of where the church is in this matter, we still must live responsible lives financially. No debts should be made that cannot be fulfilled on schedule. We must learn to go without if necessary.

We really have but a few choices. We can either live on our salary, educate the leadership and members on their responsibility to pay us a deserving wage, take a second job if absolutely necessary, or drop out of the pastorate altogether. We don't have the option to let our bills go unpaid or delinquent. Otherwise our financial reputations can destroy our effectiveness in our church and our community.

An Undisciplined Appetite

SELF-CONTROL IS A MINISTRY QUALIFICATION

Watch your life . . . closely.   —1 TIMOTHY 4:16

The man who disciplines himself stands out and has the mark of greatness upon him.   —D. MARTYN LLOYD-JONES

Have you ever noticed that many of us preachers are overweight? In fact, some are just plain obese! That could be because we are often invited to our members' homes for very fattening meals. And regularly we must go out to eat with our members and prospects for fellowship and counseling.

Eating has become an American pastime. Overeating has become a regularity with us also. Sometimes as I sit in airport terminals as hordes of people are hustling by, I can't help noticing that the majority of us are overweight. This is in direct contrast to people in other lands that I have had the occasion to visit. Outside the U.S.A. you do not see as many overweight individuals. No doubt they do not have access to the many food selections we are privileged to enjoy. But it also appears that they eat only enough to enable them to live and do their work.

Our passage instructs us to watch our lives closely. Other passages warn us against the sin of gluttony. Yet somehow we can preach against all other sins and rail against the decadent immorality around us, while at the same time exhibiting a belly that has been stuffed too much and too often. That is clearly a sin.

Perhaps we excuse it as a "little white sin" that amounts to nearly nothing at all. It seems that the two acceptable sins are worry and overeating. But God is concerned about them, or He would not have talked about them.

It is a matter of self-control. The fourth specific qualification for the office of elder/pastor in 1 Timothy 3 is "self-control." Does that involve our eating habits? You bet it does!

༾

OUR DRESS
FIRST IMPRESSIONS ARE OFTEN THE LASTING ONES

But the LORD *said to Samuel, "Do not consider his appearance or his height, for I have rejected him. The* LORD *does not look at the things man looks at. Man looks at the outward appearance, but the* LORD *looks at the heart."*   —1 SAMUEL 16:7

There is a biblical truth for which I am very thankful. That truth is that men look upon the outside, but God sees the inside. For many of us the outside is not a pleasant thing to behold. But God sees our hearts, our motives, our desires, and He knows what we are all about. Sometimes this is both reassuring and humbling, especially when that which is inside is especially dirty.

But unlike God, we are not omniscient. And we form impressions based on what we see on the outside. Others see our demeanor, our talk, our walk, and our dress.

Very little is said in the Bible about the way we should dress. Some who dressed in unusual ways—for example, John the Baptist—stood out. Of course, women are encouraged to dress modestly. And all of us are told to not cause offense, and this would include our manner of dress.

What, then, are the standards for preachers? Should we wear a thick, dark robe in the pulpit, such as we see on occasion? Or can we wear an open-neck shirt and slacks with no tie, as we find in many of the new churches of our land? What about our daily dress? Should we wear a suit and tie or, like some southern and western preachers, shirts and blue jeans during the week?

And what about the quality and cost of our clothes? Will a J. C. Penney suit suffice, or should we show up in a Jos. A. Banks suit?

There are no set, specific rules. But there are some personal guidelines. Some of them are: What is the custom of the church? How do the members dress? What can our budget reasonably cover? What standard does the general community condone? What is typically modest? What can be nice enough but not draw attention to ourselves? What is the appropriate dress for the occasion? What clothes enable us to be proper stewards of God's money?

A simple rule is: Clothes should be clean and neat, not flashy but enhancing, and should neither take attention away from nor draw attention to the pastor. Our words and walk are more important issues than our dress.

⟡

FOR ADDITIONAL STUDY

The Call

Barnabas and Saul: Acts 13:1-3
Timothy: Acts 16:1-3
Paul and the Ephesian elders: Acts 20:17-38
A general call: Rom. 12:1-8
A call and work: 1 Cor. 1:12—3:23
A trust: 1 Cor. 9:16-18
Ambassadors: 2 Cor. 5:16-21
Set apart from birth: Gal. 1:1-16
Pastors/teachers: Eph. 4:11-13
Desire and qualifications: 1 Tim. 3:1-7; Titus 1:5-9
Correction and selection: 1 Tim. 5:17-22
Final instructions to Timothy: 2 Tim. 2—4
Leadership: Heb. 13:7, 17
Serving as examples: 1 Peter 5:1-4.

Devotional Psalms (Particularly for Reflection and Praise)

Psalms 1; 8; 9; 19; 23; 24; 27; 28; 29; 30; 32; 33; 34; 36; 46; 47; 48; 63; 66; 71; 84; 86; 89; 90; 91; 96; 99; 103; 111; 113; 119; 121; 145; 150.

Our Personal Lives

The Christian described: Matthew 5-7
The greatest commandment: Matt. 22:37-40
The bondage broken: Rom. 6
Practical service: Rom. 12
Submission to and serving others: Romans 13—14
Qualities of genuine love: 1 Cor. 13
Being made alive: Eph. 2:1-10
United, serving others joyfully: Phil. 2:1-18
Rejoicing: Phil. 4:4-7
Serving as examples: 1 Tim. 4:11-16
Discharging our duties: 2 Tim. 4:1-5
Faithful examples to follow: Heb. 11
Trials: 1 Peter 1:3-9
Growth: 2 Pet. 1:3-11
Final victory: Rev. 21:1-4
Final warning: Rev. 22:18-19.

Section Two

FAMILY

LIFE

OUR WIVES

WONDERFUL COUNSELORS, CRITICS, CONFIDANTS, COMFORTERS

The LORD God said, "It is not good for the man to be alone. I will make a helper suitable for him." —GENESIS 2:18

God's wisdom is constantly being vindicated. Each day we men see the need for a helper. God was so gracious to us at the dawn of civilization to provide one. Without these special helpers constantly at our sides, we would be lonely, frustrated, overworked, and only half a person. Truly God is both gracious and wise.

For pastors, our wives are a tremendous blessing because they are in a unique position to help us in ways no other person can. Among those many ways, let's consider just four areas.

As a counselor and critic, she stands in a unique role. She knows us, she loves us, she can talk to us openly, she has our best interests at heart, and she knows when and how to approach us. She will hurt when we fail and will rejoice with us when we are successful. We should take advantage of such wonderful help. Our lives, plans, options, goals, frustrations, fears, and relationships should be open to her. She should feel perfectly at ease to serve in this capacity. We should specifically invite her to counsel and critique us often. She needs to know that we will not retaliate, rationalize, or put up defenses, but rather that we will listen to her and appreciate her.

Most wives seem to be equipped with an innate ability to pick up on small nuances and reactions that men overlook. She wants us to be wise and to do better. She is our helper. She deserves to be heard because God put her in that helping role. But she should also be listened to because she usually has something very worthwhile for us to hear.

There is another way in which she is our special helper in the ministry. She is our confidant. In our roles as shepherds, we often deal with very serious personal problems of the sheep. Sometimes it is hard to carry the burden alone. As a result there are times when we desperately need someone with whom to talk. God has provided such persons—our wives! We can trust them. We don't have to worry about the possibility that they will reveal confidential details.

Our wives also help us by serving as our comfort. Let's face it, sometimes the ministry can be frustrating and painful. Our members may disagree, disappoint, or divide themselves from us. But our wives are always there to cheer us on, to support us, to help us refocus, and to help us turn our eyes off people or events and back onto our Master.

Our wives are a tremendous blessing because they are in a unique position to help us in ways no other person can.

It is no accident that our Lord used the relationship between the husband and wife to represent His relationship with the church (Eph. 5:22-33). By using that analogy He has taught us to care for and cherish our wives. Since they help carry the load of the ministry, God wants us not only to love them but to deeply appreciate them for the special ways in which they provide us invaluable help.

I am aware that there are some pastors' wives who have not learned how to help their husbands in this way and who cannot be trusted to keep information confidential. That can be a serious problem for both the pastor and the congregation. In such a situation the pastor may need to step down until his wife has learned the value and necessity of confidentiality. She must be helped to see that great harm can come from spreading certain information. In this case perhaps the pastor's need to shepherd should primarily be to his own family until his wife is qualified for the role of a pastor's wife.

୯ᬒ

OUR HOMES
SOMETIMES THEY SPEAK VOLUMES

Now the overseer must be above reproach, the husband of but one wife, temperate, self-controlled, respectable, hospitable, able to teach, not given to much wine, not violent but gentle, not quarrelsome, not a lover of money. He must manage his own family well and see that his children obey him with proper respect. —1 TIMOTHY 3:2-4

By our homes I mean the whole package—the physical property, the organization, the size, but most important, our families who occupy them.

Two of the requirements of the pastor/elder's office are that he practice hospitality and that he manage his family well. Though he may be an excellent teacher and possess some of the character of Joshua and the patience of Job, he is unfit for the position if he is not a good manager of his home and if he does not possess the gift of hospitality.

Let's consider some of the aspects of our homes in relationship to ministry. First, the price of a house should never put our congregation under strain to support our lifestyle. At the same time, our homes should not be so stark that we are an embarrassment to the church. Neither should we put ourselves in a bind financially so that any of our bills become delinquent or that we neglect our own financial contributions to the gospel work.

Second, we know that God is not a God of confusion in His church, and we are a very important part of that body. Our homes should be characterized by order and proper decorum to the extent that we can live efficiently, redeeming the time. A home that is constantly messy and in need of repair costs us money, but more importantly costs us time that could be spent on more strategic issues. I realize that a home with small children is difficult to keep straight at all times. But even children can be taught to put away their toys, to not destroy things, and to help in other ways to keep our homes neat and attractive.

In connection with children, we are to manage our families well. We are also to lead our wives in a loving way. We are to set the tone for our families by making sure that Christ is put first in our plans, our finances, our time, and the things we talk about. It would take more space than allowed here to spell out all the possible details as to what it means to manage our families well. But it can be summarized by saying that it should be very evident to all who come into contact with the members of our families that we stand clearly with Christ and His purposes.

The last area is the hospitality of the pastor and his family. By hospitality I do not simply mean that people are invited into our homes. Hospitality involves more than giving people a place to stay and a meal. To be a hospitable person means that we draw people in and make them comfortable around us and that they perceive that we genuinely care for them.

We are to set the tone for our families by making sure that Christ is put first.

I have had the unhappy experience of staying in a home where a bed and meal were offered, but it was patently clear that the wife had no hospitable feelings toward me. That made the whole experience extremely embarrassing and uncomfortable. Quickly I moved to another setting. Had I been a lost person, I could have easily drawn the conclusion that the wife could not possibly believe what they professed as a family.

No doubt many have been drawn to Christ by the interest that godly people have shown them by opening their homes, their families, and their hearts to those who are lonely or deprived. That is a most powerful witness and is a distinct call of Christ on our lives. For the pastor, it is not only a call but a requirement.

IGNORING OUR OWN FAMILIES
ALWAYS INTENDING TO SPEND TIME WITH THEM LATER

He must manage his own family well and see that his children obey him with proper respect.   —1 TIMOTHY 3:4

You've probably heard the oft-repeated expression, "The preacher's kids are the worst on the block." What accounts for this all too familiar statement? One reason is that pastors and their families live in a fishbowl, and their lifestyle, activities, attitudes, and words are constantly being scrutinized by others, especially by unbelievers. It is expected that the pastor's family will be the example on the block; and when weaknesses are detected, often they are magnified. We have to realize that such scrutiny just goes with the territory. We are public figures, and that extends to our children as well.

It is expected that the pastor's family will be the example on the block.

But there could be another reason for the criticism of pastors' families. Perhaps they are a problem family—even the worst on the block. That can occur for many reasons, but often it is because the pastor himself, the father, the supposed example, is seldom around to minister to his own family. He is so busy preparing messages, counseling others, and meeting with the staff, elders, deacons, and committees that his days, nights, and mornings all run together. During those few hours when he is at home, he has little time or energy for his own family. After all, he has spent the last sixteen hours dealing with other families' needs. At home he is too exhausted to tackle another problem, and so his wife and children get only the leftovers.

Paul in 1 Timothy 3 says that if this is the case, we are not qualified as elders/pastors. Properly managing our own family is a must to remain in the ministry. Making our family a priority must be implemented early and systematically. This takes time and effort. If our ministry cannot be conducted in a manner that allows us the management time needed at home, we are not qualified. Our home flock is our number one responsibility. Ignoring them, or not properly caring for them, disqualifies us from the ministry!

FAMILY DEVOTIONAL LIFE
IN THE END, THEY ARE THE ONES WHO WILL COUNT!

Fathers, do not exasperate your children; instead, bring them up in the training and instruction of the Lord.   —EPHESIANS 6:4

During my ministry I have had the awesome and terrible opportunity to be in the presence of a number of people on their deathbeds. I say "awesome" because it is tremendous to be around God's people as they give testimony of their faith in the Lord Jesus Christ and of their anticipation of soon being in the very presence of God. And I say "terrible" because for many there was no commitment to Christ, and they were either hardened in their resistance to the claims of the Gospel or terrified about facing eternity. But there has never been a single case in which I heard statements such as the following: "I wish I had built a better business." "I wish I had spent more time working to build an empire." "I wish I had become a better athlete." "I wish I had spent more time traveling." "I wish my home had been larger and more comfortable." "I wish I had spent more time hunting, fishing, or playing golf."

What I most often hear is concern regarding their family. I hear from fathers who wish they had spent more time with their wives and children. They now realize that it is too late, and soon they will be completely off the scene. Their dying concern is that they let too many other things take up their time, rather than spending quality and quantity time with their families.

Though my wife and I did spend time with our three sons who are now adults, as I look back I can see that I lost a number of opportunities to know them better, to do more fun things with them, and to teach them more about the Lord. One thing that I am most thankful for is that we did have regular daily devotional times with them while they were at home. I can well remember the Bible story books we covered, the times we just opened up the Scriptures, and the times we prayed together. There were also the times we enjoyed activities like making a multiple-page list of things that would not be in heaven—no undertakers, no caskets, no tears, and no corners in schools for little boys to stand in!

Our wives and our children are our primary responsibility. Not a congregation, not a good sermon, not a well-oiled church mechanism, but the spiritual welfare of our family must come first. Then at the end of our lives there will be no regrets!

FOR ADDITIONAL STUDY

Family Life

The home:

Proverbs 3:33	Proverbs 14:1	Proverbs 19:13-14
Proverbs 11:29	Proverbs 15:6, 17, 25, 27	Proverbs 21:9, 12
Proverbs 11	Proverbs17:1-2, 17	Proverbs 24:3-4, 24
Proverbs 12:7	Proverbs 18:19	Proverbs 27:8; 29:21

Parents:

Deuteronomy 6:6-9	Proverbs 17:6, 21, 25	Proverbs 30:11, 17
Proverbs. 1:8-9	Proverbs 19:13-14, 26	Ephesians 6:1-4
Proverbs 3:1-2	Proverbs 20:7, 20	Colossians 3:20-21

Proverbs 4:1-6	Proverbs 22:6	1 Thessalonians 2:7-12
Proverbs 6:20-24	Proverbs 23:22-25	1 Timothy 3:8-15
Proverbs 10:1	Proverbs 27:11	1 Timothy 5:1-16
Proverbs 13:1	Proverbs 28:7, 24	2 Timothy 1:5
Proverbs 15:5, 20	Proverbs 29:3, 15	

Husbands:

1 Corinthians 7:1-40	Ephesians 5:21-33	1 Peter 3:7

Wives:

Proverbs 5:15-20	Proverbs 21:9, 19	Ephesians 5:21-33
Proverbs 11:16, 22	Proverbs 25:24	1 Timothy 2:9-15
Proverbs 12:4	Proverbs 27:15, 16	1 Timothy 3:11
Proverbs 14:1	Proverbs 31:10-31	2 Timothy 3:6-9
Proverbs 18:22	1 Corinthians 7:1-40	Titus 2:3-5
Proverbs 19:13-14	1 Corinthians 14:33-38	1 Peter 3:1-6

Children:

Deuteronomy 6:6-9	Proverbs 22:6	Colossians 3:20-21
Psalms 127:3-5	Ephesians 6:1-4	

Section Three

STUDY

HABITS

OUR PERSONAL LIBRARIES
WE MUST USE SHARP TOOLS

Of making many books there is no end, and much study wearies the body.
—ECCLESIASTES 12:12

Books are expensive. Books collect dust and need cleaning. Books take up much room. Books require bookshelves. Books have led many people astray. Many books are worthless, and some are downright evil. A lot of money has been wasted on inferior books.

And yet, *good* books are among the best friends a pastor can possess. Every pastor should have a solid library of study tools to which he can turn to help him know the message of the Scriptures. In fact, churches should make sure that their pastors have a book budget and should insist that their pastors purchase and use good books.

But how does one new to the ministry know which ones are good and which ones are inferior? Thankfully there are several books that will help. Here is a listing of some of them:

Badke, William B. *The Survivor's Guide to Library Research.* Zondervan, 1990.

Barber, Cyril J. *The Minister's Library.* Moody, 1985. 2 volumes plus supplements.

Barker, Kenneth L., Bruce K. Waltke, Roy B. Zuck. *Bibliography for Old Testament Exegesis and Exposition.* Dallas: Dallas Theological Seminary, 1979.

Bollier, John A. *The Literature of Theology: A Guide for Students and Pastors.* Westminster, 1979.

Carson, D. A. *New Testament Commentary Survey.* Baker, 1986.

Childs, Brevard S. *Old Testament Books for Pastor and Teacher.* Westminster, 1977.

Grier, W. J. *The Best Books, A Guide to Christian Literature*. The Banner of Truth, 1968.

Kiehl, Erich H. *Building Your Biblical Studies Library.* Concordia, 1988.

Kohlenberger, John R., III. *How to Build Your Personal Bible Library—A Step by Step Approach*. Zondervan, 1985.

Martin, Ralph P. *New Testament Books for Pastor and Teacher.* Westminster, 1984.

Rosscup, James E. *Commentaries for Biblical Expositors*. 1983.

Spurgeon, Charles H. *Commenting and Commentaries*. Banner of Truth, 1969.

Wiersbe, Warren W. *A Basic Library for Bible Students*. Baker, 1981.

Walls, A. F. *A Guide to Christian Reading*. InterVarsity, 1952.

By securing some of these volumes a pastor can have at his fingertips much information about good, sound study tools (either for purchase or on loan from a theological library). Each of the works cited above has strengths and weaknesses. If I could choose only one set to work from, it would probably be the one by Cyril Barber. Then as finances permitted, I would add as many of the others as possible.

A pastor's funds are often limited; therefore it is essential that he purchase the very best tools. Part of the value of a book is that it will freeze for all time thoughts on a printed page. Today bound books may be used a little less frequently because of the use of computer disks and the Internet. Regardless of what form they come in, good, sound, God-honoring study tools are an absolute must for our ministry. Don't accept mediocrity. We are to be craftsmen in the Word of God. Therefore we must secure and use sharp tools.

POOR STUDY HABITS
IT IS MIDNIGHT SATURDAY, AND I AM STILL CRAMMING!

Be diligent in these matters; give yourself wholly to them.
—1 TIMOTHY 4:15

It is just ten hours before I step into the pulpit for the morning message, and I'm not nearly ready. In fact, I'm petrified! I would love to find a hole to crawl into and pull the hole in after me. All week I couldn't settle on what I wanted to preach, and here I am just a few hours away from the message and just now know what my topic or passage is. There's not enough time to study the passages, make a good outline, come up with illustrations and applications, develop a riveting introduction and a powerful conclusion. Sound familiar?

For the most part, especially as a young pastor, set about to preach expository messages through books of the Bible.

Sometimes the press of counseling, hospital visits, weddings, funerals, administration, meetings, family responsibilities, and the like so crowd in on us that we find ourselves at the end of the week with little material to preach adequately on Sunday. That definitely happens to some of us, and I suspect that even the very best scholars/preachers will face the dilemma from time to time. Often it happens because we have allowed ourselves to fall into poor study habits or have not jealously guarded our time from the barrage of immediate needs, and so we come to Saturday night in sheer panic.

How do we avoid this? We cannot always avoid it. But we can set a pattern that will dramatically help, and it is fairly simple. For the most part, especially as a young pastor, set about to preach expository messages through books of the Bible. This has so many advantages that in this short space we could not list them all, but for our purpose here the main advantage is that we know weeks and months ahead what we will be covering. That eliminates one of the big battles for the preacher. Our subject has been laid out before us well in advance, and during the week of the sermon we can be studying, outlining, and planning illustrations and applications even while we are in the middle of other chores.

Carefully plan on how you are going to divide the book up sermon-wise. Get to know the book thoroughly, and let it dwell in your mind daily. This method takes some of the pressure off preparation for any one lesson because the study for each lesson helps prepare for the next one. By Saturday night you will probably only be putting on the finishing touches or simply going over your message as a last-minute review.

SPENDING DAY AFTER DAY IN THE STUDY

WE CAN LOSE TOUCH WITH OUR MEMBERS

Ministers are not cooks but physicians, and therefore should not study to delight the palate but to recover the patient; they must not provide sauce but physic. —JOHN DAILLE

A sermon is not made with an eye upon the sermon, but with both eyes upon the people and all the heart upon God. —JOHN OWEN

When I preach, I regard neither doctors nor magistrates, of whom I have above forty in my congregation. My eyes are on the servant maids and the children. —MARTIN LUTHER

Many faithful pastors will have regular study days, or portions of days in which they are not to be interrupted unless there is an emergency. This is critical because study is hard, and digging out the meaning of a passage can require some deeply concentrated time. Each pastor works at a different speed and finds a certain schedule better for his own needs.

Some who are more scholarly will relish the time spent with their books (and, now, computers) and may find that tending to the daily needs of the flock is an interruption of their schedule and their personal love of study. As their study interests grow and their library expands and their interaction with theological and philosophical positions becomes intense, some may find themselves with an overwhelming desire to lock themselves in their studies for days on end only to exit on Sunday to deliver what they have learned that week. More and more they become bookworms, and they and the congregation learn less and less about each other.

As the shepherd of the flock, the pastor must feed the congregation from the Word of God, and in order to do that he must know God's Word. But shepherding is not only feeding—it is also caring, protecting, bandaging, loving, supporting, encouraging, rebuking. Not all of this can be done from the pulpit or the study. Much of it must be done on a personal basis, one-on-one.

Shepherding is not only feeding— it is also caring

Obviously a church of any size needs several shepherds to be able to tend to the flock properly. Some pastors may be selected to do the majority of the preaching from the pulpit, while others will be given more time to shepherd one-on-one.

Even with this arrangement every pastor must have some contact with the congregation or he will grow out of touch with the people he is trying to shepherd. Perhaps in extremely large churches the preaching pastor will have only a few members he specifically shepherds, while the other pastors come alongside him to do the majority of the one-on-one counseling. Still, he must know what is going on in the body; otherwise his messages will miss the mark.

For the average church, the pastor needs to be both in the study and out among the flock on a regular basis. No set percentage of time can be given for these two areas because every pastor and congregation is different.

The key is to know both our passage and our people. Both are indispensable if we hope to address the congregation's needs.

STAYING OUT OF THE STUDY
SOON WE'LL HAVE NOTHING WORTH SAYING

The Word of God is too sacred a thing, and preaching too solemn a work, to be toyed and played with. —WILLIAM GURNALL

Some pastors are born students with inquisitive minds, while others must work very hard to develop their minds and to stay with a text and a sermon until the preparation is complete. Some love their books dearly. Others see them as necessary but difficult to master. Some could live in their studies, while others can't wait to get out of them and be among the flock. One group has a temptation to become isolated, while the other group is very gregarious. The latter group faces the temptation of spending an insufficient time with the books. They will begin to slide by in their preparation, rationalizing that their flock needs them more and more on a daily basis. Pretty soon their preparation is on a rushed, Saturday-night basis, and before they know what is really happening, they come up with little to give to their flock. They get into deep trouble as the congregation begins to starve.

A sad state of affairs emerges. The sheep are starving, but the pastor's storehouse of goods has become depleted. This calls for personal discipline and an accountability partner who will help. In such a situation, the pastor needs to have someone to whom he must name his passage, provide a general analysis, and cover the basic points in his message by the middle of the week. If he can do that, then the remainder of the week can be used for fleshing out the message.

By waiting until the end of the week to begin his preparation, the pastor has no time to devote to solid exegesis. He has no time to come up with good outlines, illustrations, and applications. His sermons are incomplete and likely a waste of his flock's time.

The Scriptures call on us to study the Word, telling us that we who teach will be judged with greater strictness (James 3:1). We are told to become approved workmen who are not to be ashamed (2 Tim. 2:15).

We are responsible for others' souls and will give an account for them (Heb. 13:17). If we cannot in time become reasonable students of the Word, we must step aside and let others take up the responsibilities of the pulpit.

MAKING YOUR STUDIES
WORK FOR YOU LATER
TIME-SAVING TECHNIQUES

To waste time is to squander a gift from God.   —JOHN BLANCHARD

There is nothing which puts a more serious frame into a man's spirit than to know the worth of his time.   —THOMAS BROOKS

The year is made up of minutes. Let them be watched as having been dedicated to God. It is in the sanctification of the small that the hallowing of the large is secure.   —G. CAMPBELL MORGAN

The great need in the Christian life is for self-discipline. This is not something that happens to you in a meeting; you have got to do it.
—D. MARTYN LLOYD-JONES

Most of us have had the experience of devouring a book, pamphlet, or article and being deeply impressed with the choice nuggets of truth we found. These were things we definitely planned to use in a message. Then we put the book back on our shelves only to discover much later that we have entirely forgotten the points we had considered so salient and useful.

Or we have heard information, stories, illustrations, and helpful outlines that would enhance messages for our listeners, but we have forgotten what we heard. Or we have read book portions, newspaper stories, magazine articles, quotations, or other stories or have recalled personal glimpses and incidents we think we could use later, only to forget about them. No doubt many of us get a handle on some of the difficult passages of Scripture, or theological or philosophical thought, only to forget the material soon thereafter. That can be both discouraging and humbling.

Some system for marking, reproducing, and/or filing this material could potentially save us many hours of searching. Today with scanners, computers, and electronic filing systems, what we now have to work with is mind-boggling.

Being able to retrieve material quickly and efficiently will be useful to us.

Whether we use only hard copies or a computer or both, the fact is, unless we employ some form of filing and retrieval system, gathering material for the occasion can be quite costly time-wise.

Whatever system or equipment we use, being able to retrieve material quickly and efficiently will be useful to us. It will be helpful to have established some very broad, general categories for material. Examples could be sermon outlines, illustrations, applications, introductory material, closing material, cities and localities, statistics, counseling material, biographical information, translation data, sermons preached (including title, passage, location, and date), major doctrines, minor doctrines, special resources, and so on. Then under those general headings, subdivisions could be added. Those divisions could still be broadened to include much finer distinctions.

For the busy pastor in our present culture, with information exploding all around us, we must have some means to harness this information in a form that we can locate and use later. With scanners and computers we can easily do so.

Pastors should start this practice early. Good personal habits in this area can save an enormous amount of time later and can both enhance our messages and speed up their preparation.

꿈

DAILY SCHEDULES
OUR HABITS, OR LACK THEREOF,
CAN DESTROY OUR EFFECTIVENESS

The surest method of arriving at a knowledge of God's eternal purposes about us is to be found in the right use of the present moment. Each hour comes with some little faggot of God's will fastened upon its back. —FREDERICK W. FABER

An old saying ("if you aim at nothing, you are certainly going to hit it") is very pertinent when it comes to daily schedules for the pastor. The tyranny of the urgent will consume our time, and when the day is gone we will have seen another day disappear without having accomplished many of our goals. A succession of such days can be disheartening.

How do we keep the above scenario from becoming an ongoing problem?

We can often avoid getting sidetracked by carefully planning our days and by frequently saying no. Urgent matters will arise where we must drop everything and give those situations our full attention. But by having other helpers in place, whether staff or well-trained laymen, we can have a congregation accustomed to seeing other leaders besides us. By making these plans we can say no ahead of time in a non-offensive manner. But back to daily planning.

Some days need to be set aside for study and contemplation. A time for prayer is crucial. Perhaps a certain day of the week should be devoted to administration (writing and answering letters, for example). Other blocks of time could be devoted to staff meetings. A time set aside for private brainstorming or long-range planning could be very useful. And of course time must be devoted to actually putting the message together. Time must also be allotted for meeting with and counseling our members.

How one arranges these times will vary. For some, the mornings, when our minds and bodies are most rested, are good times for study. For others, the quietness of the evenings is more productive.

We can often avoid getting sidetracked by carefully planning our days and by frequently saying no.

As a general rule, study and preparation should probably be done early in the week to keep us from coming to the weekend unprepared. The afternoons, after study, could be devoted to administration and counseling. Staff meetings can often be doubled up with lunch to help redeem the time. Often that is a good time to meet with members too, especially those who work. And lunch-time conferences are self-limiting as to their duration. Many members, however, can meet with you only in the evenings.

Setting a routine will help keep things moving and should help prevent daily crises from dominating our schedules. Emergencies will arise, and then we have to scrap our plans for the day; but as soon as possible we need to return to our prearranged schedules. By doing so we keep on-target with our long-range goals and are much more likely to attain them.

❧

OUR BIBLE NOTES
WHEN OUR MEMORY IS IMPERFECT

The difference between reading and study is like the difference between drifting in a boat and rowing toward a destination.
—OSCAR FEUCHT

An honest man with an open Bible and a pad and pencil is sure to find out what is wrong with him very quickly.   —A. W. TOZER

With the passing of time I am coming to the point where most people eventually arrive—some loss of memory. For things that you want to forget, that's just fine. But for those things you desperately want to remember, that's another story. We have to practice writing things down more often, if we can remember where our pen and paper are kept!

This is especially important when it comes to God's truth. Though we seem to have no problem remembering large areas and the major truths, those small matters we forget can lead to frustration.

I have always kept copious notes in my Bible, especially in the New Testament—side notes, comments between the line spacing, footnotes, notes on the edges of pages, on blank pages, and anywhere else I could write. Many times these have made a significant difference when my memory failed me. However, there was one thing that I did not anticipate. Bibles wear out. Some can be rebound, but even then the binding process can cause the loss of some important notes written on the margins of the pages. I know because I have had that unhappy experience on several occasions.

One of the greatest acts of love that my wife has ever done for me was to surprise me by taking one whole summer to copy all of my handwritten Bible notes into a brand-new, leather-bound New Testament. My Bible was literally falling apart. When I used it during messages, often some of the pages would slip out and fall to the floor. Yet I could not bring myself to give it up. I often remarked that if I lost my Bible, I would probably lose half of my theology. It had years of my detailed studies built into it. But my loving, generous wife patiently copied all of those notes into a new New Testament. Nothing I could ever do for her could match that act of love.

How should we mark our Bibles? Each person will have a different plan. There are some books and booklets devoted to this matter, and they should be consulted. But without trying to get into too many specifics, here are some general observations.

If you are not using one of the new study Bibles that automatically provide you with a lot of information, build into your own notes background information, outlines, dates, chronologies, word studies, good translations of certain words, cross-references, and general and specific ways to apply the text.

Use a thin-line, dark, permanent pen, never pencil; otherwise fading takes place. Sometimes a color-coded system in which certain colors represent particular topics, doctrines, or events can be beneficial.

Marking action verbs is extremely informative. Drawing attention in some way to the repetition of words or thoughts in a book or section is also helpful.

Sermon outlines built into our Bibles are good, especially because there will be times when we will be called on with short notice to speak to a group. If we have the outline in our Bibles, we have what we need in those instances.

It is also helpful to jot down the name of an author, a commentary, or a page number when someone has done a superb job of dealing with a difficult passage. When people ask about the verses, you can quickly refer them to a particular work.

Regardless of how you handle marking your Bible, the point is that since our minds are imperfect, and the Bible is our Book, it can be extremely helpful to retrieve quickly what took us literally hours and hours to dig out. It can be at our fingertips if properly recorded and preserved in our own Bibles.

FAXES, E-MAIL, THE INTERNET
THESE MODERN GADGETRIES—WHAT NEXT?

. . . so in Christ we who are many form one body, and each member belongs to all the others. We have different gifts, according to the grace given us.   —ROMANS 12:5-6A

I am convinced that people born before the 1950s have a serious learning deficiency when it comes to electronic equipment. To say the least, we are usually electronically challenged. When I obtain a new fax machine, a different computer, or any other new electronic gadget, the first thing I do is call one of my sons to come hook it up and help me work out the details. For a mind that is quickly fossilizing, these instruments can be bewildering.

Yet I am learning to use them because of their tremendous time-saving features. What bugs me is that just as soon as I learn how to use the thing, a new one, much faster and more complex, pops up, and I am behind the times again.

Our overall communication systems are being updated almost daily. Today's pastor must somehow try to stay up with this rapidly changing environment because we are in the communication business. We are called to communicate God's Word to our congregations and to a lost society around us. The world is communicating its message quickly and with devastating success. As Christians, especially as pastors, we have to be able to disseminate the Word of God efficiently.

Younger pastors have grown up with computers, and for them there is little problem. Indeed for some of you, this new equipment is an enjoyable fascination, quite easy to learn and use. But the rest of us need help. Apart from classes (especially interactive classes) that we can attend regularly, one of the best ways we can avoid getting hopelessly behind is to enlist the services of younger members of our congregations. This serves a twofold function. They teach us about and help us with the new electronic equipment, and their helping out in this area gives them an opportunity to be useful in the Kingdom of God.

We must stay informed about better ways to communicate. Help is often right there in our own congregations. We just need to spot those members and encourage their service in these vital areas.

PERIODICALS, PAMPHLETS, NEWSPAPERS
WE MUST NOT BE IGNORANT MEN

We do not know a millionth part of one percent about anything.
—THOMAS EDISON

You cannot find knowledge by rearranging your ignorance.
—RONALD EYRE

Our chief study must always be the Word of God. To be ignorant of this Book is to disqualify us as pastors/elders. We must never step into a pulpit or attempt to teach others unless we know both the Lord and His Word.

It is also very helpful for the pastor to know what is going on around him. Otherwise he will not know what his members are struggling with, what philosophies they are encountering, what world events they may be concerned about, and what pressures they face daily.

I have met pastors who never read newspapers, buy no magazines, and subscribe to no periodicals. Usually their pastorates were extremely small and their influence very limited. They are often out of touch with the world around them, boasting that their Book is the Bible.

Jesus knew the Word. But He also knew the world around Him. Consider His denunciation of the Pharisees, His warning to the high and mighty of His world. His knowledge of farming, fishing, sheep, households, weddings, and other customs was remarkable. In His parables and stories He used all of this information to instruct, encourage, and warn His hearers.

The local newspapers can keep us abreast of our community as well as of world events. A good magazine can cover material in more depth. A good theological journal will keep us up-to-date on current theological thought. A pastoral journal can help us sharpen our ministry skills. A book service catalog will let us know when major new books are published.

We shouldn't allow these writings to dominate our time, but when properly used, these tools can supplement what we glean from God's Word and can help us be relevant in our preaching, counseling, and shepherding.

Each congregation should give the pastor not only a sufficient book allowance but a smaller and separate allowance for subscriptions. This would encourage pastors to use this additional source material, and in the long term the church will profit from the pastor's increased awareness of what is occurring around him.

READING, WRITING, SPEAKING
THE PASTOR AS A COMPLETE MAN

An ignorant minister is none of God's making, for God gives gifts where he gives a calling.   —HENRY WILKINSON

We cannot write and speak effectively about what we do not know. So we must read and comprehend material in order to have a ministry.

For many men in the ministry there is often an imbalance between the three responsibilities of reading, writing, and speaking. The man of God obviously must also be a man of prayer, but since that has been discussed elsewhere it will not be covered here.

Some men are born with very inquisitive minds and love to gain knowledge not only in biblical areas but in many other fields. Much of their time is enjoyably spent searching out the minute details of a particular subject through books, articles, and journals. Though they have this knowledge, much of it is often irrelevant or is never used and is hence wasted. Those countless hours, though enjoyably spent in one's own understanding, may not really help the church.

This is not meant to depreciate genuine scholarship in needed areas, particularly the language and meaning of the Word of God. That time can hardly be wasted. But generally a better balance of time is needed.

Then there is the pastor who spends insufficient time in his study, yet tries to fill the pulpit. He is unprepared to bring out the fullness of the Word of God in a practical manner. He is always willing to step into any speaking assignment to rally people around the Kingdom's work. He does not shy away from speaking but thoroughly relishes the pulpit time.

And there are those who love to write. They actually enjoy writing out their messages, articles for the church bulletin, and newsletter stories and are continuously writing some book or series of articles for publication. To them the written page is the most powerful medium of communication.

Actually, a proper balance and employment of all three of these disciplines make the complete man. It is true that pastors will vary in their interest and skills regarding these three areas. But being proficient in all areas will enable the pastor to do more for Christ's Kingdom.

Although speaking (teaching, preaching, proclaiming) is biblically mandated as the most common and effective means to get the biblical message out, writing is also essential for at least two reasons:

First, writing forces us to be precise in our thinking. It forces us to take general thoughts and reduce them to specific concepts, words, outlines, illustrations, and the like.

Second, by writing we are not only influencing those who actually hear our spoken words, but by the printed page we can influence other generations. We can also reach people outside our own geographical areas. Spoken words are often immediately lost forever after the sermon is completed (unless, of course, they are taped). Written words can continue on until the Lord returns.

Early in my ministry an elderly pastor gave me some wonderful advice. He said that every pastor should be a generalist about the entire biblical message, but he should become an expert in at least one particular field or portion of God's Word. And the reason is that by becoming a recognized authority, and reducing that knowledge and skill to writing, we can affect Christ's church for many years. But as a generalist only, our influence is limited to a small group of people, in a small locality, for a very limited time.

Reading, writing, speaking—all are skills that we should seek. We need to be well-rounded men of God in order to have the greatest influence, now and in the future.

⟨꙳⟩

CONTINUING EDUCATION
GOD DOESN'T CHANGE, BUT HIS WORLD DOES

Wise men store up knowledge.   —PROVERBS 10:14

Knowledge humbles the great man, astonishes the common man,
puffs up the little man.   —ANONYMOUS

It is said that we have discovered and learned more in the last few years than has been known during all the previous years of humanity's existence. And we can see no letup in sight. The amount of knowledge is growing astronomically. Sometimes it is simply mind-boggling. It can also be somewhat frustrating since there is so much to know and the storehouse of knowledge is growing at such a rate that we are falling behind in trying to keep up with it.

We know God does not change, and neither does His truth. But in order for us to avoid falling behind in our ability to present that truth to a changing society in relevant ways, we must remain always alert.

The human race's ability to communicate knowledge is also expanding at mercurial speed. Faxes, E-mail, the Internet, and ever faster and faster computers are improving and expanding daily. Yesterday's computer is out-of-date today!

Can we just be simple men of the one Book in our modern culture? As a man in his sixties, sometimes I want to throw in the towel and say, "Lord, I can't keep up with all these whiz kids who keep coming up with these gadgets. My mind just does not function that fast. It is too old and tired."

How can we present the old truth in a current form to a constantly changing audience? That's the question! In fact, that's the question John Stott attempts to answer in his very helpful work *Between Two Worlds*. In this book he does an outstanding job of giving us some very practical suggestions on how to take the truth declared in an ancient culture and give it to our modern world.

He also gives us some excellent suggestions on how to keep our minds sharp and active, such as forming discussion groups of outstanding men in various fields who will come together with us regularly to discuss current topics, movements, and thought in an open forum.

We should involve ourselves in continuing classes, seminars, retreats, and conferences that will stimulate us and keep us up-to-date on the thoughts and patterns around us.

Certain television programs, news magazines, and periodicals can keep us aware of the world around us as well. It would be very helpful to select sources that summarize well and analyze thoughtfully so we do not have to spend hours getting small amounts of data.

Obviously, we should know more about the Word of God than anything else. We are to be men of the Book, but we must also be informed about the world around us if our message is to be fresh and relevant.

FOR ADDITIONAL STUDY

The Word of God

Deuteronomy 4:2	Proverbs 13:13	Luke 11:28
Deuteronomy 6:6-7	Proverbs 16:20	John 8:31-32
Deuteronomy 17:14-20	Proverbs 30:5-6	John 14:23
Joshua 1:8	Isaiah 40:8	John 15:7
Job 23:12	Isaiah 55:11	Ephesians 6:17
Psalms 1	Jeremiah 23:29	Colossians 3:16
Psalms 19:9-11	Matthew 4:4	2 Timothy 3:15-17
Psalms 37:31	Matthew 24:35	2 Timothy 4:1-5
Psalms 119	Mark 4:14-20	Hebrews 4:12
Proverbs 2:6	Luke 8:21	

Section Four

MESSAGES

TOPICAL MESSAGES
OUR MESSAGE MUST EXPOSE GOD'S TRUTH

Do your best to present yourself to God as one approved, a workman who does not need to be ashamed and who correctly handles the word of truth. —2 TIMOTHY 2:15

There are many different types of sermons. Among them are the topical, biographical, textual, expository, and others. Often we will fall into a pattern that uses only one of these types, the topical sermon.

There is nothing inherently wrong with a topical sermon, as long as the message is true and meets a genuine need. There have been some outstanding topical messages preached by outstanding preachers through the years. Some of these sermons have lived on for many years and continue to bless myriads of God's people.

But there can be several problems with preaching *only* topical messages. First, it places most of the burden on the preacher to decide what God's people need to hear. In contrast, expository messages, working verse by verse systematically through the Scriptures, accept the wisdom of God who inspired His Word and who knows what His people need.

While it is true that even when preaching expositorily the pastor must make some judgment as to what he emphasizes in a passage, generally in expository messages the passage covers more directly the biblical emphasis. In either case, topical or expository, the Word of God must come through clearly.

Second, topical preaching forces the pastor to spend time continuously coming up with new topics rather than spending time with a passage itself, digging out the thoughts and the applications that God has already determined are needed (such as is done when one is involved in expository preaching).

It is true, though, that a good topical sermon is one where the pastor has spent considerable time and effort to dig into the passages referred to in order to support his message. No sermon—topical, biographical, or otherwise—should be devoid of sound biblical preaching.

Third, the congregation usually does not know ahead of time what portion of God's Word is going to be dealt with and thus they are not given the privilege of getting into the Word ahead of time in anticipation of the message.

And fourth, as a general rule, topical preaching does not teach the congregation to know how to interpret and apply the Word for themselves. Relying only on topical preaching often leaves the congregation without the tools to be students of the Word themselves. They become too dependent on the preacher and are often starved for the Word of God.

Solid, exegetically correct, expository preaching should be the main diet, with some topical, some textual, some biographical, and other types of messages sprinkled in where needed to keep the sermons relevant, interesting, and informative. Such a rich spiritual diet will cause both the pastor and his congregation to grow.

TONE OF VOICE
IT CAN HELP, HURT, SOOTHE, ENCOURAGE, ANGER, BE MISUNDERSTOOD

Ministers must so speak to the people as if they lived in the very hearts of the people; as if they had been told all their wants, and all their ways, all their sins and all their doubts. —THOMAS BROOKS

When love is felt, the message is heard. —JIM VAUS

The same command "stop that," given by a mother to her unruly child and then later lovingly to her husband as he gently tickles her ribs, conveys a totally different message due to the tone of voice.

It has been my observation over the years that some preachers, while in the pulpit, use the same tone throughout the message. Some are totally serious, and their tone is extremely tense. Others are harsh and demanding, and their listeners cower in fear. Some present the message in a meek and mild manner, while others employ tears that often leave the congregation slightly embarrassed. Some are totally didactic and logical in their presentations, and often the congregation reacts as if attending a college class.

The human spirit contains our minds and our emotions. Our emotions should never be allowed to rule over our minds. We see too much of that today in what I would label "mindless Christianity." That eventually leads to hazy theology and ultimately into mysticism.

Our emotions should never be allowed to rule over our minds.

But God did give us emotions, and rightly controlled, they are there for our good. As public speakers and as private counselors, we must be aware that both the mind and the emotions are always at work in our listeners. And these emotions are challenged, angered, encouraged, or cheered not only by our words but also by the tone of our voice.

Imagine John the Baptist having come like the meek and mild Casper Milquetoast. His ministry would have been about as effective as trying to fight off an angry bear with a wet noodle. Or imagine Jesus talking to the woman who had been caught in the act of adultery, speaking to her in a harsh, angry, and threatening tone.

In the same message or counseling session, there will be a time to speak softly in an encouraging way, there will be times to present truth in a straightforward manner, and sometimes we will use an authoritative but loving tone when calling on people to repent.

There is no way to cover all of the possible examples, but a general maxim is to vary our tone according to the specific subject and audience. But remember, the tone must always be genuine and must be suitable for the topic we are covering and the occasion on which it is delivered. The tone must come from our hearts, not from theatrics contrived to move people.

This will not only help us be effective both in and out of the pulpit, but it will also let our congregations know that we are concerned for their souls and that we love them personally. Keep in mind that they don't particularly care how much we know, as long as they know how much we care! Tone of voice can demonstrate our care.

Too Much Time on Exegesis
IT CAN FAIL TO MOTIVATE PEOPLE

It is one thing to learn the technique and mechanics of preaching; it is quite another to preach a sermon which will draw back the veil and make the barriers fall that hide the face of God. —James S. Stewart

Preaching is theology coming through a man who is on fire.
—D. Martyn Lloyd-Jones

It is vital that pastors know the message of the Word of God. This is critically true if we stand before a body to tell them what a passage is saying. We need to have gone over and over the text, paying particular attention to the background, the context, the type of literatures, the meaning of the words, the nuances of the original language, the person, tense, mood, and voice used, and an analysis of the leading commentaries.

As an illustration of this, it is also necessary for a skilled medical doctor to have done a great deal of preparatory work. He must study test results and technical information in order to diagnose and treat our physical illness. It is not necessary or even helpful for him to tell us in excruciating detail all that he has learned about us and our illness. That is preparatory to his treating us. We want to know that he has investigated and what he has concluded. We don't need all of the technical data.

I have seen preachers enter the pulpit and go word by word through the text, explaining in great detail, giving various commentaries' views, continuing through the text line by line, but not being able to get their listeners to really understand the passage. People in the audience are copying down all of these details, trying to learn what the preacher has learned, but are not able to see the forest for all the trees. When he has completed his sermon he sits down thinking he has done his job.

Is that all we are supposed to do in the pulpit? Are we simply to explain the text in a complete and detailed manner as well as we can? Or is there more to it?

In the New Testament there is a fine distinction between teaching and preaching. The preacher is described as more of a "herald" (see 1 Tim. 2:7; 2 Tim. 1:11). He is to herald forth the good news, much as a town crier would enthusiastically announce good news. Good teaching will have some aspects of heralding about it, and it should involve some motivation and application. Good preaching will certainly involve teaching also, but preaching does not stop there. Preaching also involves a dynamic that strongly calls for action, whether it is a call to repentance and faith, a call to service, or a call to carry the Gospel to others.

When one teaches through a text, which is sorely needed today since there is so much ignorance of the Word of God, he is giving needed instruction. But if he is preaching, he must forcefully call for a response, such as we see Jesus doing in the Sermon on the Mount. And he must hold people's attention if his study and preparation are to accomplish any good.

We have been called not only to teach, but also to preach so that the Word of God can rebuke, teach, and train others in righteousness. God has so ordained preaching that it includes the dynamics of a person, his voice, and his personality. So teach in the pulpit, and preach in the pulpit. Do both at the same time. Both are required, and both are desperately needed from our pulpits today, especially good, solid, interesting, enthusiastic preaching.

SERMONS WITH NO STRUCTURE
IT'S EASY TO GET LOST IN A MAZE

It is no easy matter to speak so plain that the ignorant may understand us, so seriously that the deadest hearts may feel us and so convincingly that contradictory cavillers may be silenced. —RICHARD BAXTER

Probably we've all tried to work our way out of a maze. Perhaps we have done it with a pencil starting at Go, eventually finding our way through all of the openings and exiting at the proper spot. It would have been easier if we had been provided a set of instructions or if there had been a well-defined structure that had led us along the way.

A sermon can be a maze also. A preacher may read a passage of Scripture, pray, and then begin talking. At some point he realizes his time is up, and he closes the message. During that time his hearers have no idea how much progress is being made, what point he is driving at, and no idea when the conclusion will be reached. The reason? There is no discernible structure or outline.

It is true that too much stress can be made of the outline itself, with no real meat in the message. That is wrong also. Striving for clarity, however, cannot be overemphasized.

You've probably heard this advice before: "Tell them what you are going to tell them, tell them, tell them what you have told them, then sit down." That's not bad advice. Often we do not catch and retain matters if we hear them only once. Proper repetition is valuable. One of the most effective ways to let people know what you are attempting to get across is by way of a simple outline, which may need to be stated more than once. As for general content, it is often best to say the same thing in several different ways rather than using the exact words each time.

Many pastors like to alliterate to help themselves and the listeners remember the structure. That's fine, but not always necessary, though some structure is definitely needed. If we want our congregation to stay with us, we must let them know that we are making progress in the message and are heading to a conclusion (which often is the application). If we do so, they will more likely hold out to the end. If they tune us out because they don't know where we are heading, as someone has remarked, we are only up there foolishly flapping our bicuspids!

ﺳﻲ

SERMONS WITH TOO MANY POINTS
A STRONG CENTRAL POINT IS MORE OFTEN NEEDED

Let the preacher hold before him, through the whole preparation of the sermon, the one practical effect intended to be produced upon the hearer's will.   —R. L. DABNEY

Perhaps at one time or another you have listened to a speaker who had a very detailed outline including many points, sub-points, and sub-subpoints. Probably you found that after a while trying to keep up with all his points got you totally lost in his outline. You kept thinking, "Where is he going? What is his point?"

Structure is needed in any type of verbal address. That structure can take many forms and still be legitimate. But our limited minds can absorb only so many items; after that we become overloaded with information.

The telephone companies usually stop with seven digits because their studies show that the mind can easily remember that number of figures. Even bank account numbers try to limit the digits to seven or less. That being the case, preachers should take note. That's one reason many good preachers will only have three, five, maybe up to seven points. A few good, strong, well thought out outline points are much better than a large number of lesser divisions.

The world of carpentry is a good example for us. Sometimes a board will call for a number of smaller nails, but generally if you want to keep the board in place, one or two larger nails are a whole lot better and much harder to dislodge.

Sometimes smaller sub-points are helpful and genuinely needed to explain finer points in a message, but that should be the exception. Fewer but stronger points can more easily be carried in one's mind.

For example, let's suppose a speaker has a total of fifteen small divisions in his message. And then suppose another preacher has only three very strong points. Which sermon do you think could be more easily digested and remembered? We are in the communication business to get God's message across to men and women. Good communication principles must be known and used in the pulpit if we are to accomplish our purpose.

❦

SERMONS WITH
NO DISCERNIBLE POINT
SO WHAT, PREACHER?

It is but poor eloquence which only shows that the orator can talk.
—JOSHUA REYNOLDS

There were a lot of interesting illustrations in that message. It was full of truth. The preacher really exegeted the Scripture passage well. He had a powerful introduction that made us take note of what he was about to say. Initially we were riveted to our pews. Some of his illustrations really moved us, one even to tears. But we never quite got the point of the message.

If another member were to ask what the preacher was talking about, we might have great difficulty summarizing it in one sentence. We could remember the Scripture passage. We could retell some of his stories, especially the funny ones. The one that moved us to tears will always be with us. We could probably recall some of his outline. But somehow we failed to get the real point of the message.

That should never happen when our congregation leaves on Sunday. As they are leaving the sanctuary, they should be able to restate the main point of the message. In fact, we want them mulling it over and over in their minds.

Is it that we are telling them they need to repent and be saved? Is it that we are telling them they must uphold the unity of the body? Is it that the Scriptures can be totally trusted? Was our message designed to get people to serve unselfishly in the church? Were we trying to get across to the congregation that their witness on the job is crucial?

As they are leaving the sanctuary, they should be able to restate the main point of the message. In fact, we want them mulling it over and over in their minds.

We see this principle in Jesus' preaching. At times His one point was that we must forgive others, or that there is great rejoicing in heaven when a sinner repents, or that the Kingdom of Heaven is worth our forsaking all. He did not try to get across a whole series of important truths every time He preached. His hearers left with His one main point ringing in their ears. And they seldom missed it. Some went away sad, hurt, upset, angry, or rejoicing, but they went away having understood the point Jesus had made.

Sometimes it is appropriate to state, "The point of this message is . . ." and then develop the thought. That forces the preacher to determine in his own mind exactly what it is that he is attempting to get across to his listeners. If he cannot do that for himself, he should not expect his hearers to be able to know what he is saying.

SERMONS WITH
NO ILLUSTRATIONS
I COULDN'T QUITE UNDERSTAND WHAT
THE PREACHER WAS SAYING

"But we had to celebrate and be glad, because this brother of yours was dead and is alive again; he was lost and is found." —LUKE 15:32

Almost every Christian around the globe can identify the source of the above words. "Why, sure, they're the concluding words of the parable of the prodigal son." In fact, they are the conclusion of what has often been called the greatest sermon ever preached.

The sermon contains three well-known parables—the lost sheep, the lost coin, and the lost, prodigal son. When we examine this sermon we find little didactic teaching. Most of Jesus' teaching was by telling stories about well-known events, customs, animals, types of people, and the like. His truths hung upon examples that most could understand.

People can learn better when you attach truths onto something with which they are familiar.

People can learn better when you attach truths onto something with which they are familiar. Teaching parabolically is extremely effective. Unfortunately, none of us will ever come up to the teaching standards of our Lord. Our attempts at parables would for the most part be very limited.

But there is a way to get truth across, if used properly. And that is by using good illustrations. Illustrations, properly employed, are windows that let the light shine through to a congregation's mind. They should never be used to call attention to themselves, but only to illustrate (throw light on) the truth.

Illustrations also create interest and help hold attention. Have you ever listened to a speaker, and his didactic points begin to fade in your mind, and then he says, "Let me tell you a story" or "Let me illustrate what I am saying"? I'll bet your mind suddenly relaxed and your interest perked up.

If the illustration clarifies the subject and helps move the listener to the appropriate action or thought process, it has become a very legitimate way of getting God's truth across.

᠆᠊᠊᠊

SERMONS WITH
TOO MANY ILLUSTRATIONS
I ENJOYED THE MESSAGE,
BUT I DIDN'T LEARN ANYTHING

What is the chief end of preaching? I like to think it is this: it is to give men and women a sense of God and his presence.
—D. MARTYN LLOYD-JONES

Illustrations are great. They serve as windows to let the light in. When properly used, they make our points and applications clear. And every good sermon needs one or more of them. It pays many dividends to keep a ready source of illustrative material on hand when preparing a message. Material can come from personal experiences, newspaper articles, current local, national, and world events, helpful books or lists of illustrations, the Scriptures themselves, as well as from a host of other sources. Part of our responsibility in preparing helpful messages is to gather and use these materials.

But we have all probably sat through sermons in which a series of illustrations was used that did nothing but tell good stories. Very little, if any, truth was clarified with these illustrations. The message was enjoyable to sit through, often eliciting smiles, laughter, empathy, or even tears. But when the sermon was over, we had really experienced little but an hour of entertainment.

Jesus used illustrative material constantly, but always with a serious message attached. He used stories, events, and other material effectively to draw attention to the truth He was enunciating to His hearers. And His point was seldom missed.

At times preachers use illustrations to draw attention to themselves, to liven up their message, or to get a laugh. There is nothing wrong with godly humor in the pulpit, but it has no value if it stops there. Illustrations must be used to get our message across, and if they do not, we have wasted part of a valuable preaching hour.

SERMONS THAT DRONE ON AND ON
WHY DOESN'T HE FINISH HIS MESSAGE AND LET US GO TO LUNCH?

Seated in a window was a young man named Eutychus, who was sinking into a deep sleep as Paul talked on and on. When he was sound asleep, he fell to the ground from the third story and was picked up dead.
—ACTS 20:9

The mind can only absorb what the seat can endure. —ANONYMOUS

Some might say that Paul's message killed Eutychus. It is difficult to know whether or not this is a case of Luke's humor when he says that Paul preached "on and on." The passage tells us that Paul "kept on talking until midnight" (v. 7). But it also tells us there were many lamps in the upstairs room that probably did create some heat, and possibly gases, which would cause someone sitting upstairs to get a bit drowsy.

It is altogether possible that Eutychus was a slave and had

worked hard all week, even on the first day of the week. Possibly his body was very tired, the sermon was long, the heat and fumes were just too much for this young man, and he finally went to sleep, falling from the upstairs window to the ground below. Paul did go to Eutychus, wrap his arms around him, and announce that he was alive. Either he wasn't mortally wounded, or, more probably, Paul quickly restored him to life.

Unfortunately, we preachers today do not have the ability to exercise life-restoring power on our listeners. So our sermons must not drone on and on. We've all sat through long, boring sermons and quite possibly have delivered them ourselves! While not actually having killed our listeners, we have killed their interest in listening to the Word of God. Howard Hendricks says that if you are going to bore people, bore them with something else rather than the Word of God.

We've all sat through long, boring sermons and quite possibly have delivered them ourselves!

What causes such sermons? Lack of clear points, lack of preparation, lack of a well thought out conclusion are among the many answers. But often it is because the material we have studied is so interesting and helpful to us that we can't bear the thought of leaving some of it out. We want to give *all* of it to our congregation and thus we overestimate the ability of our listeners to stay with us.

We thus move to the point of diminishing returns, and sometimes past it. I have tried to sit through several messages with a pastor who had very few communication skills but who felt he was called to preach. His attempt to communicate was to go longer and longer, often to the point where his listeners actually became very angry with him. He not only went past the point of diminishing returns—he drove his members completely away. The church eventually folded.

Charles Spurgeon once said that one had to be an extraordinary speaker to exceed thirty-five minutes. Now don't get me wrong. I don't believe in sermonettes for Christianettes. I do believe we must have the time to explain and apply adequately a reasonable portion of God's Word. But if we do go for forty-five minutes or longer, we had better be good. We had better know where we are heading. We must speak clearly, forcefully, using good illustrations and clear applications, driving toward a good conclusion. If not, we are probably wasting our time and the time of our listeners. And we are boring people with our attempt to handle the rich Word of God. Sometimes we could even be making them downright angry!

<hr>

ADDRESSING IMPLICATIONS ONLY
SOME SERMONS ARE INCOMPLETE

Our people do not so much have to have their heads stored as to have their hearts touched, and they stand in the greatest need of that sort of preaching which has the tendency to do this. —JONATHAN EDWARDS

Preaching is exegeting, outlining, interpreting, analyzing orally, and explaining passages of Scripture. It is crossing the barrier between the culture in which the original words were penned and the culture in which the sermon is delivered. Preaching is also rebuking, cheering, encouraging, and directing others. It is to be gentle and strong, timely and timeless, encouraging and exhorting, and teaching and heralding all at the same time. That's what makes good preaching difficult, but when a sermon contains all of these elements, provided the Spirit of God is active also, men and women, boys and girls are moved to change.

In sermon preparation we must keep a number of points in mind. We must visualize our audience, know what they are struggling with, be alert to their level of understanding, and plan our messages to meet them where they are.

A passage may contain very obvious messages to the listener. In the parable of the man who was forgiven an enormous debt (probably equivalent to our $10,000,000) but who refused to forgive his debtor a paltry $20 debt, the call to us is very clear. We have been forgiven much; therefore we are to be quick to forgive others of their small sins against us. Narrative and parabolic passages are typically easy to grasp.

In other biblical literature such as the New Testament letters, the average layman may find it difficult to glean the practical application. Therefore, the preacher's duty is to bring out the implications and resulting admonitions. That places the responsibility on him to make certain that he has drawn out the correct implications from the text and that the admonitions or applications can properly be made from those implications. Otherwise, the Scriptures are being misused in those instances.

We must always put ourselves in the place of our members. Many of them are not careful Bible students and find interpretation and application somewhat difficult; therefore, they need us to show them the way.

Some pastors seem to think that providing only the exegesis and implications of the text is sufficient in a message, and that the listeners should be able to make application for themselves. But often hearers need to know specifically what to do about what is implied by the text.

We can't assume that we can provide all of the possible specific applications that our listeners should obey. But we can certainly include some applications to help the listeners think about additional specific ways to apply the passage.

To leave our audience only with exegesis and implications is to deliver two-thirds of a sermon. We need to show them how to apply the text. Jesus certainly did so. He told Zacchaeus specifically what to do to demonstrate genuine repentance. In His Sermon on the Mount, specific applications are interwoven throughout the message. He tells us how to pray, how to respond to enemies, how to turn away from the things of this world, and how to store up rewards in heaven. His sermons are a model for us, and we should study them carefully in order that our messages might also move people to proper obedience.

PULPIT NOTES
DON'T LET NOTES ON A PAGE SMOTHER YOUR FIRE

When people sleep in church maybe it's the preacher we should wake up. —ANONYMOUS

Something of the quality of enthusiasm must be in every man who preaches. He who lacks it cannot be a preacher. —PHILLIP BROOKS

Some preachers ought to put more fire into their sermons or more sermons into the fire. —VANCE HAVNER

Heart preaching inflames the spirit to worship; head preaching smothers the glowing embers. —RICHARD FOSTER

Some of the most effective and well-known sermons ever preached were read in their entirety from the pulpit. Others were preached by pastors who used very extensive notes. In some cases very influential speakers have used only a few notes hastily scratched on a note card or on the back of an envelope. Still other outstanding messages were delivered by those who had no pulpit prompts or helps of any kind, having only their Bibles in their hands.

Therefore, there can be no set rule as to how much material we should take into the pulpit with us. Each pastor will have his own methods and varying skills. Some methods require copious notes, while others need only limited helps. However, in recent years there has been a significant change in our listeners' ability to sit through and absorb our sermons, which may affect the notes we carry into our pulpits.

This change has occurred as a direct result of television. Our hearers' ability to concentrate on spoken material has been significantly altered. Along with words, people are now accustomed to seeing images. And along with images they are used to frequently changing variety. Whether we like it or not, the fact is that we must now work doubly hard just to hold their attention through a message.

With no images and little variety, they begin to shut down mentally, assuming a glazed stare, their minds elsewhere.

I want to emphasize that the Holy Spirit can and will work when He wants to, in whom He wants to, how He wants to, and in whatever situation and style of sermons He wants to. He is sovereign. He can take the worst message, homiletically, and use those words to convert and change people's lives for eternity.

Yet in a very real sense, God has worked and still works through the art of preaching, using men's natural abilities, homiletical styles, skills, and personalities to bring souls into His Kingdom. And for that reason our preaching needs to be effective. How, then, in our TV-influenced culture can we effectively deliver the truth of God?

As for content, there must be good introductions, relevant subjects, truth, logic, progression, cohesion, and strong and directive conclusions. For good delivery, several important ingredients are needed more today than ever before.

- *Good audience contact* is essential. More is needed than just eye contact. The audience needs to know that we are speaking directly to each of them. At times eye contact is sufficient, but at other times movement away from the pulpit itself to one side of the podium, then the other is helpful. This necessitates our looking up from our notes and moving away from those notes and toward the audience. By our eyes, our voice, our gestures, our actual place on the podium, the congregation needs to realize that we are talking to each one of them.
- *Life stories* will almost always stir up our hearers' interests. They are much better told than read. They must always help to make our points, not just be a filler or attention grabber.
- *Encouraging audience participation* by asking questions and getting verbal responses helps break down some of the barriers and secures the listeners' attention. God has for many centuries used monologue style preaching. But today

it seems that at least some form of dialogue is becoming more effective. Great care should be taken in asking for audience participation. Questions must be appropriate, causing the audience to think and become involved in the message.

• *Appropriate humor,* as long as you are driving to a serious conclusion, is a good way to help your audience relax and be drawn into what you are saying. Humor in bad taste and only for humor itself is not good. One very effective speaker has said that if he could get his listeners' mouths open with something humorous, then he could pour some spiritual medicine down their throats.

• *Describing things in a way that legitimately moves people,* even to tears when appropriate, will help them stay with you. This should never be artificial, but God has given us emotions, and properly stirred, they can be very useful. Some of the most effective messages I have ever heard are those in which I both cried and laughed. The real test is whether or not the truth was preached, and in those messages where I heard God's message, my emotions were stirred in both directions, and I hung onto every word.

• Where possible, *a change of mood and method of presentation* several times during the sermon is helpful, when legitimate, so that the shorter (TV-trained) attention spans can more easily handle the material being developed.

• Perhaps it would be beneficial to add *a clear, short statement of points* in a conclusion so the listener can later recall (and perhaps discuss) what was taught.

To summarize, to be ourselves in our pulpits and to reach our modern audiences, sometimes we will use notes extensively, and other times we'll just speak from our hearts. Our goal should be to help the audience become one with us as we deliver God's truth.

᷂

BALANCING TRUTH
A HALF-TRUTH IS NOT A TRUTH

A thousand errors may live in peace with one another, but truth is the hammer that breaks them all in pieces. —CHARLES H. SPURGEON

It is very easy for preachers to begin riding hobbyhorses. Without realizing it we may begin to emphasize a particular biblical truth in almost every message. Sometimes we may think this particular truth has been so neglected by the general Christian public that it is our duty to stress it often before our congregations. Or perhaps we are so impressed with this portion of God's message because it has spoken so strongly to us personally that we want others to be equally moved.

Then there are those biblical truths that must be balanced because left to themselves they represent only half of God's heart and message. God's total sovereignty over the will of man is a good example. This is a truth explicitly taught in Scripture; however, there is another truth that balances it out—the scriptural presentation of man as a creature who is ultimately and totally accountable for his actions. God's sovereignty and man's moral responsibility are two parallel truths that should never get out of balance in our ministries. Otherwise we will represent only half of God's message.

Other examples of needed balance are God's wrath and God's love for the sinner. Some pastors preach in a way that leaves people with the idea that all God looks forward to is punishing sinners in a fiery hell. Others present God's love so often, with no mention of wrath, hell, and eternal punishment, that people feel sorry for God because though He is trying his best to love people, they thumb their noses at Him, and there is nothing He can do about it. An overemphasis on God's love has also caused some to believe that there is no real hell and ultimately everyone will be saved.

Law and grace are other areas that we need to balance in our preaching. God is a righteous judge, and He will see that all of the demands of His law are met. He is also a God of grace who offers forgiveness and complete pardon on the basis of Christ's atoning sacrifice through faith in Christ as one's Savior. Law and grace should receive equal emphasis in our preaching.

A final example involves messages dealing with the preservation of the believer (sometimes referred to as the security of the believer, or once saved—always saved). In some circles that truth is presented so often that people do not recognize there is a balancing truth taught in the Bible, that of the perseverance of the saints. Those who are genuinely saved are absolutely secure in Christ and will never be lost. But for those who have adopted an easy-believism and who exhibit no fruit of genuine repentance and conversion, there can be no security. They must persevere in godliness in order to demonstrate that they are truly Christ's sheep. The preacher must constantly emphasize both truths, without the exclusion of either.

We should continually reassess our messages to make sure we have not emphasized one side of God's truth but neglected the other. Probably the best antidote for this is to preach systematically through books of the Bible. In so doing we trust God to create the proper balance for us as we properly exegete and apply His truths as they are encountered in the pages of His rich Word.

FAILING TO SHARE THE PULPIT
YOUR CONGREGATION DESERVES SOME VARIETY

When pride comes, then comes disgrace, but with humility comes wisdom. —PROVERBS 11:2

Regardless of how good a thing is, we have a tendency to grow tired of the same-old same-old. Familiarity does breed contempt. I can't think of a better candy bar than a Snickers. But I wouldn't want Snickers for breakfast, lunch, and dinner for weeks and months on end. That principle applies to the pulpit also. In many pulpits today, for forty-eight to fifty weeks a year the congregation must listen to the same person, hear the same voice, listen to the same pronunciation, view the same gestures, often hear the same stories, lessons, and examples, sometimes twice on Sundays and again on Wednesdays. People tire of hearing the same thing over and over.

Now some preachers are so qualified and equipped that they can hold an audience much longer and more often than others. But they are rare indeed. Even with those who are immensely qualified in the pulpit, many of their members thoroughly enjoy a substitute from time to time. Yet there are some preachers who seem to fail to understand this and think that because their members still sit there and listen to them week after week, they are ministering to their needs. The truth is, though the parishioners continue to come, mentally they are absent.

Why do some pastors want to be in the pulpit, if not all the time, at least most of the time? Perhaps they do not have a reasonable replacement, and they shudder to think of someone else filling the pulpit. But there may be a couple of other reasons. Could it be that some think they are that good and that they can only accomplish their goals by filling the pulpit week after week, with no break for themselves and for their congregations? Despite their view on this, could there be others on the staff or in the congregation who, if given an opportunity for a more public ministry, could minister effectively and perhaps even grow beyond the one pastor?

In either case the reasoning is flawed. Why? First, we must constantly be on the lookout for other men who could be groomed for the ministry. And there is no way to determine if they are suited for the position unless we give them the opportunity to demonstrate their gifts and talents. And second, variety really is good at times. To think that people profit only from us is to ignore a basic need of humans.

We need to give ourselves regular breaks. And we need to give our congregation frequent breaks from our voices. Obviously this could be taken to excess, but with proper, planned rotation we could get some R and R, our members might just liven up a bit, and others might be developed and drawn into an ever dwindling crop of suitable pastoral candidates.

Don't let either fear or pride stand in the way. Jesus trained others to follow. John the Baptist said that he must decrease while Christ must increase. Paul was constantly preparing those who would continue after him and who, in turn, would train others, who would train still others. We must not let this cycle be broken. In discipling others, our attitude should be that we will have great satisfaction and joy as we see our disciples far exceed our own gifts, abilities, and success in the ministry.

We have a tendency to think of the pulpit as "my pulpit." In truth, it is Christ's pulpit, and we are His servants—but not His only servants! He may be preparing great men right in our midst. Let's give them a chance to succeed in a public ministry also, and if they grow well past our own abilities and audiences, God's people will be blessed, God will be pleased, and we can rejoice.

⟜

TRANSLATIONS
ALL THESE MODERN VERSIONS!

A thousand times over the death-knell of the Bible has been sounded, the funeral procession formed, the inscription cut on the tombstone, and committal read. But somehow the corpse never stays put.
—BERNARD RAMM

If we were pastoring before the 1950s, we might have expected that the vast majority of our congregations today would be using the same translation we were reading then, the *King James Version*. Today in almost any church body there may be ten or more different translations being used by the members in the same preaching service.

That places a bit of a burden on us as we prepare our messages, especially if they are textual or expository in form. We will be asking the people to look at specific verses and particular words in those verses. Often the particular choice of words can have radically different meanings. So we need to know what translation the majority of our congregation is using in order to know what needs to be addressed.

Today in almost any church body there may be ten or more different translations being used by the members in the same preaching service.

Most often the pastor's choice of a translation will be what many of the members will bring to church. There will be a substantial number of people, however, who will stick to a translation of their own choice. Some of them will not recognize the difference between a translation and a paraphrase. Others will not be aware of the constantly changing nature of any spoken language and will not know about the subtleties of the languages. So part of our responsibility will be to educate our congregation regarding different translations of the Bible.

This education can take different paths. A message or two or a class or two could be given on just what is involved in translating the Scriptures, explaining the reasons we must have translations. Another approach would be to note those occasions when there are significant textual problems in a passage, point out how translations differ, and briefly discuss the science of biblical translation.

Regardless of how it is approached, with so many translations in use today, we must be aware of this matter and educate our members. This will involve a public endorsement of some translations, publicly raising some cautions about others, and warning our members about those that are significantly inferior.

When preparing messages on texts and why the better translations differ substantially on their choice of words or phrases, it would be helpful to explain why there are differences, to evaluate these variances, and to state our preference, citing reasons for doing so. This not only enhances the understanding of the passage under discussion but also provides a specific analysis of the several translations in use by the body.

Dealing with a problem text could be an occasion to announce that although we normally use a certain translation, we prefer another one at this point because of its superior rendering. Our purpose should be to help the congregation come as close as possible to the original words, to understand their context, and then to apply and obey the intent of the original language.

FOR ADDITIONAL STUDY

Sermons and Messages

Nathan: 2 Sam. 12:1-14.

Solomon: 1 Kings 8:54-66.

Jesus: Matthew 5—7; Matthew 10:1-42; Matthew 11:7-30; Matthew 12:1-50; Matthew 18:1-11; Matthew 15:3-5, 23:1-39; Luke 11:17—12:12, 22-59; Luke 17:1-37; Luke 20:27-47; Luke 21:8-38; John 3:1-21; John 6:25-59; John 8:31-47; John 10:1-38; John 14:1-31; John 15:1—16:33.

Peter: Acts 2:14-41; Acts 4:8-12; Acts 11:4-18.

Stephen: Acts 7:2-53.

Philip: Acts 8:26-40.

Paul: Acts 13:16-48; Acts 16:29-34; Acts 17:16-34; Acts 20:17-38; Acts 22:1-29; Acts 23:1-10; Acts 24:10-26; Acts 26:1-32; Acts 27:21-26.

The message: Mark 16:15; Acts 17:18; 1 Corinthians 1:23; 2 Corinthians. 4:5; Ephesians 3:8; 2 Timothy 4:2..

Sermons: Jesus' Use of Parables, Stories, and Illustrations

Notice the constant use of a wide variety of illustrative material:

Fish and fishermen: Matthew 4:19; Mark 1:17.

Salt: Matthew 5:13; Mark 9:50; Luke 14:34-35.

Light: Matthew 5:14-16.

Moths and thieves: Matthew 6:19-20.

Eyes: Matthew 6:22-23.
Birds and lilies: Matthew 6:25-34.
Plank: Matthew 7:1-5.
Dogs and swine: Matthew 7:6.
Stones and serpents: Matthew 7:7-12.
Two gates: Matthew 7:13-14.
Sheep and wolves: Matthew 7:15.
Thorns and thistles: Matthew 7:16-20.
Two houses: Matthew 7:21-27.
Foxes and birds: Matthew 8:18-22.
Physician and bridegroom: Matthew 9:10-15.
Old garments and wineskins: Matthew 9:16-17.
Sheep and harvest: Matthew 9:36-38.
Sheep and wolves: Matthew 10:1-28.
Sparrows and hairs: Matthew 10:29-31.
Swords and crosses: Matthew 10:32-38.
Reed and clothing: Matthew 11:1-15.
Children: Matthew 11:16-17.
Sheep and pits: Matthew 12:10-13.
Trees and fruit: Matthew 12:33-35.
Jonah, the Queen of the South, and Solomon: Matthew 12:38-42.
Empty house and evil spirits: Matthew 12:43-45.
The sower and the seed: Matthew 13:3-23, 36-37.
Tares and wheat: Matthew 13:24-30, 36-43.
Mustard Seed and birds: Matthew 13:31-32.
Leaven (yeast) and meal (flour): Matthew 13:33-35.
Treasure hidden in a field: Matthew 13:44.
Merchant and pearl: Matthew 13:45-46.
Good and bad fish: Matthew 13:47-50.
Scribes and householder: Matthew 13:51-52.
Uprooted plant: Matthew 15:12-13.
Blind leaders: Matthew 15:14.
Dogs: Matthew 15:21-28.
Weather forecasting: Matthew 16:1-4.
Leaven (yeast): Matthew 16:6-12.
Rock and keys: Matthew 16:15-19.
Mustard seed: Matthew 17:19-21.

Millstone and lost sheep: Matthew 18:1-14.
Unmerciful servant: Matthew 18:21-35.
Camel and rich man: Matthew 19:16-26.
Landowner and servants: Matthew 20:1-16.
Fig tree: Matthew 21:17-22.
Two sons and vineyard: Matthew 21:28-32.
Landowner and heir: Matthew 21:33-46.
Marriage feast and garment: Matthew 22:1-14.
The burden of the Pharisees: Matthew 23:1-4.
Blind guides: Matthew 23:16-24.
Gnat and camel: Matthew 23:24.
Cup and platter: Matthew 23:25-26.
Whitened graves: Matthew 23:27-32.
Vipers: Matthew 23:33.
Chicks under a hen's wings: Matthew 23:37-39.
Lightning: Matthew 24:27.
Carcass and vultures: Matthew 24:28.
Fig Tree: Matthew 24:32-36.
Thief: Matthew 24:36-44.
Faithful servants: Matthew 24:45-51.
Ten virgins: Matthew 25:1-13.
Talents and rewards: Matthew 25:14-30.
Sheep and goats: Matthew 25:31-46.
Lamp and light: Mark 4:21-22; Luke 8:16-17.
Seed and harvest: Mark 4:26-29.
Master and porter: Mark 13:34-36.
Creditors and debtors: Luke 7:41-43.
Good Samaritan: Luke 10:25-37.
Friends at midnight: Luke 11:1-10.
Snakes and scorpions: Luke 11:11-13.
Rich Fool: Luke 12:13-21.
Watchful servants: Luke 12:35-48.
Barren fig tree: Luke 13:6-9.
Oxen and the Sabbath: Luke 14:5-6.
Guests at a wedding feast: Luke 14:7-11.
Giving a feast: Luke 14:12-14.
A great banquet: Luke 14:15-24.

Building a tower: Luke 14:25-30.
A king going to war: Luke 14:31-32.
Lost sheep: Luke 15:1-7.
Lost coin: Luke 15:8-10.
Prodigal son: Luke 15:11-32.
Unrighteous steward: Luke 16:1-13.
The beggar Lazarus: Luke 16:19-31.
The mustard seed and the unprofitable servant: Luke 17:1-10.
Unrighteous judge: Luke 18:1-8.
The Pharisee and the tax collector: Luke 18:9-14.
Profitable and unprofitable servants: Luke 19:11-27.
Water and wind: John 3:1-13.
Living water: John 4:1-42.
Bread: John 6:35-58.
Living waters: John 7:37-39.
Day and night: John 9:4.
Door, gate, sheep, shepherd, thief: John 10:1-21.
Grain of wheat: John 12:23-26.
Many mansions: John 14:1-46.
Vine, vinedresser, fire: John 15.
Woman in travail: John 16:20-22.

Section Five

CHURCH

LIFE

CANDIDATING BEFORE A CHURCH
WE MUST BE PAINFULLY OPEN AND HONEST

Do not be hasty in the laying on of hands, and do not share in the sins of others. Keep yourself pure. —1 TIMOTHY 5:22

It takes a long time to get to know people well. For that reason it is a good practice for a church to grow its own elders/pastors. By that I mean that the congregation should seek to be aware of those men in its midst who may think they are being called into the ministry. As these men are recognized by the congregation, they should be given the opportunity to teach and to lead ministries within the local body. If they meet the biblical qualifications, have a desire for the ministry, and prove themselves over a period of time, the church will then be in a position to observe their progress and formally ordain them.

This enables the church to select men who have proven themselves as they have lived before the congregation. It takes time to know a person's fitness for the ministry, to know his theology, to know how he responds to different situations, to know his personal walk before the Lord, and to know how he might shepherd the flock. Perhaps an elder/pastor training program would be helpful in which the person serves unofficially in that role until the church has opportunity to assess the person's overall qualifications.

This close relationship is not always possible. In some situations congregations find themselves with men who either do not desire the leadership or with men who are not qualified for the ministry. In that case outside candidates must be sought. While certain background and reference checks can be made, men whose qualities are unknown are often brought before the congregation. If we are pastoral candidates, we must be painfully honest. We must be completely open about our weaknesses as well as our strengths.

This process of choosing men from outside the congregation has often caused undue pain for both the candidate and the church. When men have been chosen who are not right for a church, after a few months it becomes apparent, and either there is a breakup of the relationship or the disillusioned pastor continues on with an unhappy church.

The remedy is to take whatever time is necessary initially to make sure all available information is on the table. The theological positions must be matched. The preaching style, pastoral objectives, methods, and worship form must be acceptable. The salary and benefits must be clearly agreed upon. The pastor's family must be known. If there are any lingering problems in the church, they must be laid bare before the candidate. If there are any major sins, weaknesses, or failures in the pastor's background, they must be clearly known by at least the search committee. In other words, there must not be any skeletons of any kind in any closets. Eventually they will come out; so they must be brought out early so everything may be examined, checked on if needed, and laid to rest.

If we are pastoral candidates, we must be painfully honest. We must be completely open about our weaknesses as well as our strengths.

It is also important for the candidate to interview the leadership of the church. He needs to know them personally, their leadership style, their expectations, both the church's strengths and weaknesses, and the leaders' vision for the church's future. Becoming one of the pastors means he will be joining that leadership team, and he needs to know if it is a team with which he is in agreement.

It can only hurt the candidate and the church when a pastor is chosen and either one later realizes it was a mistake. This happens too often. Complete, up-front disclosure is the only way to minimize the likelihood of this tragedy occurring.

LEADING, NOT FOLLOWING

SHEEP NEED SHEPHERDS

A leader has been defined as one who knows the way, goes the way, and shows the way.   —ANONYMOUS

When I was growing up, for a period of time my family lived in a semirural area. For some unknown reason stray dogs would find their way to our property and make it their home. Since some were female, we would often have a litter of puppies to deal with. One particular female stands out.

Her litters of puppies were always large, and dealing with a large number of growing dogs was not our idea of enjoying life. After several pregnancies we decided we had to do something. So early one morning we loaded her into our 1939 automobile, took her into town, through town, and all the way to the other side of town, leaving her near the city dog pound, approximately twelve miles away from our home. That day we shopped, visited, and returned home late in the evening. Much to our astonishment, that dog was standing on our front porch, happily wagging her tail, awaiting our return. She had found her way home all the way from the other side of town and could not wait to greet us. How she did that, I'll never know. Our hearts melted, and we gave her a permanent home from that day forward. Dogs can be extremely intelligent (and persistent!).

But sheep do not respond that way. It has been said that you could lead a flock of sheep from your front yard to your backyard, and on their own they could not again find the front yard. They would need a shepherd to show them the way. That's their nature (their limitation, actually). God knows the nature and characteristics of sheep. He made them. And that is the way He describes us as His people. Just as sheep need shepherds to lead them, God's spiritual sheep (the church) need spiritual shepherds to lead them into truth and righteousness. Ultimately Jesus is the great Shepherd, but He has chosen men to be His under-shepherds to pastor the flock.

The relationship between spiritual sheep and their shepherds illustrates many points, but here we will talk about only one area— spiritual leadership. In His design and providence for the church, God has established leadership—plural leadership. The type of ministry and government in each local church will determine if and how this leadership will function.

For some bodies almost every issue is put to a vote by the congregation, and the elected leaders merely carry out the will of the sheep. In some cases even though the leaders may significantly disagree, they are bound to carry out the decisions of the congregation. In my opinion, that is following, not leading. If that had occurred during Moses' day, the Israelites would still be in Egypt, under bondage, eating garlic, leeks, and onions.

We cannot sit back and wait for the sheep to lead. A few will, but by and large they are looking to us for direction, feeding, and leadership by our stepping out courageously in faith.

Real leadership involves working to be out ahead of the congregation in knowledge, wisdom, plans, courage, and faith. Joshua was a prime example of this, as was the apostle Paul; the greatest shepherd is our Lord Himself.

We cannot sit back and wait for the sheep to lead. A few will, but by and large they are looking to us for direction, feeding, and leadership by our stepping out courageously in faith. If there is a collection of leaders such as a group of elders (which is the biblical pattern), there is a built-in set of checks and balances to help ensure that the flock is not being led in the wrong direction.

When a congregation has an unbiblical form of government that prevents the established leadership from leading, the pastors must patiently and systematically teach the body the proper form of church government. To try to lead without the members understanding their role to follow can be both frustrating and ineffective. To change an unbiblical situation may require a lengthy series of messages to establish God's order for His church. In doing so it must be made clear that elder *rule* and congregational *involvement* are not to be considered mutually exclusive.

Leadership involves taking bold steps forward, not simply reacting. It involves courage and the ability to take occasional spiritual lumps. It involves faith in a sovereign God and a trust that His Word works. It involves a sacrificial love for the flock, a love that will move us to lay down our lives for God's people.

As we lead we will feed, protect, encourage, warn, correct, and help heal those who are hurting. We will not sit back waiting for the flock to be the vanguard. *Shepherding means leading.*

TRYING TO DO IT ALL
THE SHEEP ARE CALLED TO A MINISTRY

It was he who gave some . . . to be pastors and teachers, to prepare God's people for works of service.   —EPHESIANS 4:11-12

Some pastors are worked to death. They may teach a class, preach all the messages, lead all the services and meetings, handle the office chores, prepare the Sunday bulletin, do most of the visitation, make the hospital calls, do all the funerals, weddings, and counseling, represent the church in all social activities, and coach the softball team. Before long they suffer from burnout.

That is not God's design for the church. The pastor in this situation usually has no one to blame but himself. He has failed in his duty. His responsibility is not to do it all himself but to "prepare God's people for works of service." Sometimes it seems quicker to do all the chores himself than to have to talk people into taking on specific tasks or responsibilities, train them, and then follow up to make sure they have carried out the assignments. We've all had situations where members have promised to take care of certain matters, and we learn later that they did not follow through. With some pastors, that has created a desire to do it all to ensure that things are done properly. But ultimately this just means that less will be done because one person can be stretched only so far.

A pastor who tries to do it all himself . . . is not fulfilling the duties of his ministry.

It is our duty to enlist, educate, train, and demonstrate by example what church membership is all about. One person has commented that there should be no drones in God's church. We are told by God's Word that every person has been given one or more gifts and that those gifts must be exercised for the good of the body (Rom. 12:4-8). As leaders we, along with the board of elders, should be assessing the gifts of our members, matching them up with potential areas of service, assigning tasks to them, and encouraging them in their work. Members need to hear it emphasized that we were bought with a price, the blood of Christ, that we are not our own, but rather that our gifts and abilities have been given for the good of the body of Christ.

Some pastors may feel threatened by members who have been trained or educated to serve with excellence, perhaps even better in some respects than the pastor. But rather than feeling that way, the pastor must instead be grateful for those believers' gifts and qualifications. If he has done a good job of teaching them and providing leadership, well-functioning members are evidence of a successful ministry, rather than an occasion for jealousy on his part.

A pastor who tries to do it all himself, who cannot recruit, train, and delegate assignments to others, is not fulfilling the duties of his ministry (Eph. 4:11-12). We are to prepare God's people for their ministries, not do it for them.

❦

MEETINGS, MEETINGS, MEETINGS!
NECESSARY, BUT THERE CAN BE TOO MANY

Never futile is the work of the church, for it is a product not of the
mind of man but of the sovereign grace of God.

—WILLIAM HENDRIKSEN

As I prepared to retire formally as the executive pastor of our church, I was asked what I would miss most and miss least about the ministry. As for the most, I stated that I would greatly miss the daily interaction and accountability of my fellow pastors and the church body. Though my plans were to continue as a member in the same congregation (after a brief time away), I knew that my time with the pastors and members would be significantly diminished. And I would greatly miss those times together.

As for the things I would miss the least, I simply said, "Meetings, meetings, meetings."

We had weekly staff meetings, weekly elder meetings, weekly discipleship meetings, monthly deacon meetings, monthly finance committee meetings, monthly mission committee meetings, monthly relocation meetings, monthly Care Group leaders' meetings, budget meetings, various communications meetings, congregational meetings, and too many others to mention. Many of them met early in the mornings (5:30 to 7:30 A.M.), while others met in the evenings.

As the executive pastor, I was involved in almost all of these meetings. Some weeks I was at it by 5:30 or 6:00 three or four mornings a week. Then I was out late at night during the evening meetings. Sunday morning, Sunday evening, and Wednesday evening services would come along, in addition to other special weekly activities. Eventually the whole process began to take its toll.

Yet it is crucial for the welfare of the church to have constant, open communication. The team must know what is going on, and everyone must be operating from the same playbook.

As the church grows, more and more areas can be delegated to others. That should be the goal of leadership, so that no one or two individuals are worn out from attending all of these meetings.

There are a few matters that must be insisted upon when these meetings occur. If done, they will cause the meetings to be more productive and to be attended more faithfully.

There must be a chairman who will actually preside over the gathering. The meeting must start on time and end on time. A well-planned agenda must be sent out ahead of time. The chairman must be able to keep the agenda on track. He must be able to appoint sub-committees when needed. He must be strong enough to correct those who get off the main subject, be able to table things when needed, and end the meetings on time.

It is crucial for the welfare of the church to have constant, open communication. The team must know what is going on, and everyone must be operating from the same playbook.

God is not a God of confusion, especially in His church. When meetings are needed and properly held, He is glorified, and the church benefits. But meetings should always be under proper scrutiny by the leadership to make sure they are required and helpful.

Meetings for meetings' sake are harmful. They wear people out physically. They can be occasions for differences and hurt feelings and divisions. But when they are carried out in the proper spirit, with proper leadership, they can bring glory to our Lord and can be good for our congregations.

❧

HOUSE CALLS
INDISPENSABLE IF WE ARE TO KNOW OUR SHEEP

"You know that I have not hesitated to preach anything that would be helpful to you but have taught you publicly and from house to house."   —ACTS 20:20

To love to preach is one thing—to love those to whom we preach, quite another.   —RICHARD CECIL

Richard Baxter's *The Reformed Pastor* is a must-read book for all pastors and elders. In this book Baxter demonstrates what a pastor must do to shepherd the souls of his parishioners. There is too much in the book to try to summarize here. Purchase a copy of this important work. Live with Baxter for several months. You'll be both humbled and challenged by the pastoral work of this man of God.

In this section I want to emphasize just one point of Baxter's work—shepherding from house to house. Our times are different, members are more scattered than in Baxter's time, and the demands upon pastors are more diverse. But Baxter's concept of going into people's homes deserves our attention. How Baxter closely shepherded 700 to 800 people is still a mystery to me, but he apparently did so consistently, and effectively. By calling on his members regularly in their homes, he could see firsthand how his members lived, could meet the entire family, and could talk to people in their most relaxed times. While there, he rebuked those in sin, encouraged the downcast, and discipled and catechized those who were weak in the knowledge of scriptural truth and the doctrines of the faith.

Today it is both easier and more difficult to make house calls. It is easier in that larger churches usually have multiple pastors on staff who can divide up the responsibilities of shepherding. It is also easier now due to rapid transportation.

But several factors make it more difficult today. Because of rapid transportation, members often drive long distances to attend services. In our own church, people drive from a few blocks up to almost fifty miles. To visit everyone in their homes will require that we use much of our available time traveling. Also, the role of shepherding has unfortunately changed in that the pastor/elder is now living in a more complex society, and his time is often taken up with a myriad of duties. It seems that the vast majority of Baxter's time was spent in his members' homes shepherding their souls.

Today we should earnestly work to effect two changes. We should seek to delegate many of our extraneous duties so that we are available to shepherd members' souls. And we should divide the responsibility for families in the congregation among the pastors/ elders so that frequently one or more of us is in our members' homes taking care of this important duty.

Also, the time before and after Sunday services could be used for short conversations to check up on those who need to be encouraged (or challenged) as well as for making appointments when issues require more time or intensity. The telephone is a wonderfully efficient way of maintaining beneficial contact, and with the advent of e-mail, communication with many members has taken a further step forward.

In the area of shepherding, an ounce of prevention is certainly worth much more than a pound of cure. Perhaps some members or their children do not have a genuine grasp of the Gospel or have a faulty theological understanding, are wrestling with depression or are struggling with particular sins. These are things that we will never know if we see them only as they sit in the pews.

There is one final very minor suggestion I would make to those who visit members in their homes. Most people will want to make you feel welcome and will exhibit courtesy toward you. Part of that process is offering you something to drink, such as coffee, tea, or a soft drink. Often I have been invited to have a piece of cake or pie with them. Many times I have been asked to stay for a meal. Sometimes to refuse these offers makes them uncomfortable; so try to take something. If not some of the above, tell them you'll take a glass of water. Accepting something from them will help them relax around you. This is a very small issue in view of the totality of your purpose, but it can help the atmosphere of your visit.

Home visits can clearly demonstrate to our members that we care for them and that we take seriously our responsibility as the shepherd of their souls.

༜

HOSPITAL VISITS
THERE ARE GOOD WAYS, AND THERE ARE BAD WAYS

I venture to say that the greatest earthly blessing that God can give to any of us is health, with the exception of sickness. Sickness has frequently been of more use to the saints of God than health has.
                                                    —CHARLES H. SPURGEON

Sickness, when sanctified, teaches us four things: the vanity of the world, the vileness of sin, the helplessness of man and the preciousness of Christ.   —ANONYMOUS

If you have ever been in a hospital, possibly facing a long-term illness or serious surgical procedure, you know what it means to have wonderful visits from others. On the other hand, you may have had visits from those whom you wish had not come. The difference had to do with how good or bad you felt, how well or not so well you knew the visitor, and how well or not so well your visitor knew how to make hospital visits. Such visits can be wonderful or excruciating times. What do we need to think about as we make hospital calls? Here are some random thoughts based on more than forty years of experience.

• Know the person's name, condition, prognosis, and spiritual condition, if at all possible. Sometimes the answer to those questions cannot be readily ascertained. But often with a few calls to others we can know those matters before we enter the room. By having that information we can know the direction in which to take the conversation.

• Our goal should not be to entertain the patient by simply talking about family, the weather, or sports. There are many more important things to talk about, especially when there is a serious illness or upcoming surgery.

• Respect the condition of the patient. When that person is hurting or very uncomfortable, do not stay long. You are only placing a wedge between you and the patient when you drone on and on while he lies there wishing you would leave so he could rest.

• Never sit on patients' hospital beds. Causing movement of their bodies can unintentionally hurt them. And often they are self-conscious about their bed clothing and the odor of their breath. Allow them some space.

• Give them an opportunity to express themselves. Ask them gently if there is something about which they would like to talk. Sometimes they are fearful about their lives or need to confess some things they have said or done. If you do all of the talking, they cannot or will not bring up these matters.

• If others are in the room, be careful that you do not embarrass the patient by talking about intensely personal matters, by asking inappropriate questions, or by demanding responses. If necessary, ask the others if you could have some time alone with the patient, then address such matters privately. If necessary, come back at a later time.

• Always pray for and/or with the patient. God is the real physician. He can heal both the soul and the body.

• Leave the patient with an appropriate but brief passage of Scripture. This may be just what he needs to meditate on. A marker at that point in a Bible or some verses written out on a card or piece of paper could be very helpful.

• We should remember that we are on the physician's turf, and we should respect the doctor/patient relationship. If needed, we should excuse ourselves and never impose ourselves upon their discussions.

• If the patient is not someone you have known or who has known you, leave your card in the event the patient or the family decides to contact you in the future. Through the years this has often been the beginning of a long-term, spiritual relationship between the pastor and the patient and his family. What starts out as a hospital call may end up a rich spiritual blessing for all. In fact, sometimes just being there (even when few thoughts are expressed) may produce fruit later.

• Our visits should never appear only as professional duties. If the patient perceives that we are there only to carry out our responsibility, rather than having a genuine concern for him or her, our visit can do more harm than good.

᠀

FELLOW PASTORS/ELDERS
WE DESPERATELY NEED THEM

The reason I left you in Crete was that you might straighten out what was left unfinished and appoint elders in every town, as I directed you.
—TITUS 1:5

Both in the Old and New Testaments we find our Lord calling and sending out men to do His work, not alone, but with a helper. It was Moses with Aaron, Joshua and Caleb, David and Jonathan, Paul and Barnabas, later Paul and Silas, and Paul and Timothy, to mention a few.

Obviously in each case there was a leader among the leaders. But seldom were they alone. There are probably a number of reasons why the Lord chose to provide helpers and companions to come alongside His servants.

Leadership can be very lonely because ultimate and final decisions sometimes isolate those who have to make them. It can be a very lonely task to sort through options, choose a proper course, and seek to get others to help implement it. Knowing that some of the followers will question or disagree with the decisions is very trying on those who must chart the paths. Having fellow leaders and companions around us can provide needed wisdom, correction, and support. These checks and balances can help prevent major leadership errors.

We also need those around us who will help keep our theology correct by constantly challenging our positions. This can be accomplished as we study together and talk about our conclusions. We will gain help from others as they recommend works for us to read. As they teach and lead, we can learn from them. And as we teach and preach, they can spot our deficiencies or those times when we have failed to communicate properly with the congregation.

A leader also needs the regular accountability of other men who are on the same level with him. As I write this paragraph, the leading world news story is President Clinton's impeachment. I can't help but think that the course of our nation's history would have been different had President Clinton been open to several accountability partners who were straightforward and honest with him.

As pastors we will be held up to intense scrutiny and criticism. Many times this scrutiny will be good for our souls, but other times it will be unfair and will cause us deep pain. It is especially important to have our fellow pastors/elders come alongside us to help lift our spirits and encourage us to stay the course.

Perhaps these are some of the reasons the New Testament always speaks of a plurality of elders in local churches (Acts 14:23; 15:6, 23; 20:17; 21:18; 1 Tim. 5:17; Titus 1:5; Jas. 5:14; 1 Peter 5:1). In no instance do we find a *single* pastor/elder leading a New Testament church. God's design for His churches is a plurality of leadership.

Too often we see churches with a single pastor and a board of deacons. If those are the only called and qualified men in the church, we should not force other men into an office for which they are not suited. But our goal should be to have a sufficient number of men in the office of elder so that God's design for His churches will work.

To try to serve as the sole leader in a church is much like trying to raise a family as a single parent. It can be done, but it is not God's design and is not usually healthy for the biological family or for the church family.

How do we correct this matter of solitary leadership? We must continually make it a priority to seek out and disciple men who exhibit leadership qualities and gifts.

DEACONS
THE CHURCH'S GOD-GIVEN SERVANTS

"Brothers, choose seven men from among you who are known to be full of the Spirit and wisdom. We will turn this responsibility over to them and will give our attention to prayer and the ministry of the word." —ACTS 6:3-4

Deacons, likewise, are to be men worthy of respect. . . . They must first be tested; and then if there is nothing against them, let them serve as deacons. —1 TIMOTHY 3:8-10

Whether the men in Acts 6 were the first deacons can be debated, but the 1 Timothy passage makes clear that deacons are needed in each of God's local bodies. Elders serve by leading; deacons lead by serving.

I was raised in a denominational church in which there was a single pastor and a board of deacons. The deacons were looked upon by the congregation as the leaders of the body. They hired and fired the pastor. They made the decisions for the body. They drew up the budgets, spent the church's money, determined when congregational meetings were held, set the agendas, and were viewed as those who held the church together. The pastor was considered little more than a hired hand who was somewhat dispensable and often replaced.

But obviously that is not the proper role of deacons according to the New Testament. Elders are to be the spiritual leaders. Deacons are to serve the body. That is what the word *deacon* means—"servant." This does not mean deacons are to have no spiritual qualities. In fact, in 1 Timothy 3 the qualifications for the offices of deacon and elder are the same except for one. The elder must be apt to teach; that is not required of the deacon.

Elders are to be spiritual leaders. Deacons are to serve the body.

Among their roles, deacons can handle the church finances, look after the building(s) and grounds, provide for proper facilities for worship, teaching, and edification of the body, look after the widows (and widowers) and orphans, and assist the pastors/elders in a number of ways to enhance their spiritual oversight. The deacons are to be spiritual men who have a heart to serve and who clearly know the Word of God. But their role is not to be the spiritual leaders. That role is for pastors/elders.

As pastors part of our responsibility is to teach the congregation what qualifications we should look for in men who may serve as deacons. And we should be encouraging such men who have servants' hearts to step forward and offer to serve.

God's church functions very well when it runs on His tracks, when pastors/elders lead properly and deacons serve wholeheartedly and faithfully.

There will be deacons who serve with such spiritual excellence and who exhibit such leadership qualities and abilities to teach that we will want them to join us in a leadership role as elders. They will have been trained as servants and will be in a good position now to serve as leaders. Their qualities will have been demonstrated to the congregation and to the leaders, and it will be quite natural to move them into the eldership.

CHURCH FINANCES

KEEP YOUR DISTANCE!

*Two-thirds of all the strifes, quarrels and lawsuits in the world arise
from one single cause—money!*   —J. C. RYLE

One of the quickest ways for a pastor to raise needless questions about
his integrity, to become burdened with things unnecessary, and to be
tempted to treat members with partiality is to become involved in the
church's finances. Though the elders are ultimately responsible, the day-
to-day financial affairs are best left to the deacons.

That does not mean the pastor should be totally in the dark about
budgets, goals, overall income and expenditures, and other general
information. But being involved in the weekly nitty-gritty of the
church finances can take him away from the job to which he has been
called.

Certainly he should suggest to the boards those areas to which
church funds should be directed. For example, he should lead his congregation to support foreign missions, inner-city projects, ministries
to the poor, pastoral training centers, book and tape ministries, legitimate parachurch ministries, and many others. As a faithful expositor of the Word, he should lay before the membership and the boards
the biblical mandates and the opportunities presented to be involved
in these gospel ventures. His sermons should highlight those areas
needing support. But collecting, recording, and forwarding the money
given should never go through his hands. His reputation should never
be put at risk.

Pastors are human and sometimes may be tempted to find out
who gives and who does not or the amounts people give and may
even want to compare others' giving with their own. That's not a
good practice and can become legalistic. I am aware that some
would disagree with me on this point, saying that an elder should
be aware of the sheep's stewardship. But I am unmoved by their

arguments. Try as we might, the size of a person's contribution can easily stick in our minds and can influence our messages or our practices at some later date. If we were not sinners, perhaps knowing specifics about how our individual members give would be something we should know. But being sinners, I am afraid that we would be facing too many temptations to be partial to certain members of the flock.

Perhaps those who are selected as officers should be open to some form of accountability in this area. One of their responsibilities is to be an example to the flock, and certainly financially supporting the church is one of those areas in which a leader's qualifications should be tested.

Some people will want to place gifts directly in the pastor's hands. Some will do this to encourage the pastor, while others will do it to be recognized. Regardless, the pastor must never reveal the donor's name and gifts unless instructed by them to do so.

I have had the above occur a number of times in my ministry. Gifts have been placed in my hands, from a few dollars to several thousand dollars, and one for several hundreds of thousands of dollars. When the latter occurred, it was very tempting to want to shout it on the housetops to encourage the remainder of the church. But I was requested to keep the name and amount confidential. In cases like that, we must simply rely on God who will appropriately bless both the giver and the congregation.

"The love of money" is truly "a root of all kinds of evil" (1 Tim. 6:10). It is not money, but the love of it that is a source of temptation. By not becoming involved with the finances on a regular basis we can remove that temptation before it ever begins. Our duty is to preach about money at the proper times, to pray that our members will respond as God wants them to, and to encourage our deacons to handle both the incoming and the outgoing money to the glory of God.

THE TELEPHONE
A NECESSARY PROBLEM

Ministry that costs nothing accomplishes nothing.
—JOHN HENRY JOWETT

No man's life is for his private use.   —ANONYMOUS

Just like a doctor's, the pastor's telephone can ring at any time day or night. And just like the doctor, he is on call twenty-four hours each day.

In larger congregations where there are multiple pastors, a rotation system can be set up for pastors to be on call. But for the average church (which accounts for the vast majority of churches in our country), there is only one pastor, and he is on call all the time, day and night. His phone can literally ring at any time for every imaginable reason.

Some are using answering machines to regulate their calls and to provide some downtime away from the demands of the pastorate. But ultimately calls must be returned, and though they can be grouped, work is still left to be done. To some members who are desperately facing urgent matters that they need to talk over with their pastor, a faceless, nameless, answering machine message can be cold and disappointing.

I have known of some pastors who developed a reputation of not returning calls except to those to whom they felt particularly close or in whom they had a personal interest. Fairly soon such a lack of response begins to catch up with such pastors, and their ministries get into trouble. Their members lose trust in them and begin to drift away, feeling that their pastors really do not care about them.

Some calls will be serious, even urgent—an unexpected death, an accident of some kind, a marital separation, serious illness, loss of a job, discovery of marital infidelity, a family member's repudiation of the faith, or some other emotional trauma. When our members are facing crisis times like these, they do not need to hear the emotionless voice of a recorded message.

So how do we solve the dilemma of the phone ringing constantly (placing us on call at all times) when we are faced with the need for extended concentration on our studies, a reasonable time for R and R, and uninterrupted time with our families? There are no perfect solutions. But here are some thoughts.

When members know that their pastors really do care for them, they will understand that there are going to be times when they are unavailable. The pastor must work hard to establish that fact in his members' minds. That can only be done by daily caring for their souls by deeds done, not by simply saying words. Then when circumstances make him unavailable at a particular moment, they will not presume he is not interested in their welfare.

Obviously if there are enough pastors, the rotation system is a very practical way to meet this need. But if the congregation is small, the pastor can train some of his elders or even "lay elders" or deacons to handle occasional emergencies. At a minimum they could at least provide some initial counseling until the pastor's schedule allows him to take over.

Another possible solution is for the pastor to leave a recorded message that gives the times he will be available and directs the caller to other spiritual members of the congregation. Though this is not ideal, it does avoid the pitfalls of a recorded message that simply says the pastor is not in, leave a number, and he will return the call when he can.

The goal is to let the members know that he is genuinely concerned to help them in their struggles. By demonstrating his love and concern, he can help hurting members to be better able to deal with their difficulties. Also, his counsel should be wise and helpful as he directs their minds to what the Word of God says about their problems. Obviously there is much in the Word of God to which the pastor can direct them, and that, above all, should be his objective.

Phone calls from hurting members, though sometimes tiring, are good. They demonstrate to us that there is a shepherding relationship going on. And that, after all, is our calling. We should become concerned if our phone stops ringing!

SCHEDULES AND APPOINTMENTS
THEY REQUIRE FLEXIBILITY IN THE PASTOR'S LIFE

*One's mere word should be as trustworthy as a signed agreement
attested by legal witnesses.*   —CURTIS VAUGHAN

There are no degrees of honesty.   —ANONYMOUS

In several respects a pastor's and a mother's work are alike. Their work is never finished. There are always things yet to be done. Their daily schedules can be completely interrupted without notice. In the case of a mother, a sick child can destroy her plans for the day. In the same way, a sick, grieving, or hurting church member can set aside the pastor's plan for his day.

A pastor's schedule is very difficult to maintain, especially when he has a growing congregation. Though he may strongly desire to have specific days and times for study, staff meetings, prayer, visitors, and hospital calls, it is simply unrealistic for him to think he can always maintain that schedule without interruptions. There are just too many irregularities in the ministry. Emergencies are part of the norm.

With those factors a definite part of the pastor's life, there are times when he will feel he must get away from it all, cancel his appointments, catch his breath, and regroup.

There is nothing wrong with the pastor taking some well-deserved R and R. And when he needs it, he must notify his staff, elders, deacons, and members that he needs a rest. They should be made aware of the many demands on his time and energy that necessitate a change in his schedule.

There will be times when he must be straightforward with his congregation and let them know that his schedule is too full to meet some of their needs. And there will be other times when he should cancel appointments previously arranged. But when doing so, he must be completely honest with those involved.

When there are congregational emergencies, such as a sudden marital breakup or an unexpected serious illness, appointments must be broken. Without compromising confidentiality the pastor should explain that the broken appointment is absolutely necessary.

Such times can be opportunities to educate the congregation as to the role and work of the pastor. He can also encourage the flock to pray specifically for his needs, wisdom, stamina, and overall judgment as he handles these unexpected emergencies.

We should also seek to learn creativity and efficiency in the skills of handling appointments and meetings so as to use our time well and thereby make the most of the day.

Interruptions are part and parcel of the pastor's life, and he needs to be able to flex with the situations his ministry presents to him.

꿎

DIARIES/DAILY PLANNERS
THEY HELP KEEP US ON TRACK

Laziness and frivolity are bad enough in any profession, but worst of all in that of a watchman for souls. —J. C. RYLE

The pastor who has been in the ministry for some time has more than likely forgotten appointments, speaking engagements, special services, seminars he had signed up for, special events he had agreed to attend, members' surgery dates, weddings, rehearsals, and other activities he definitely planned to attend.

Sometimes we are like the absentminded professor. We can carry deep theological discussions in our brains but cannot remember to take our umbrellas in a rainstorm. We receive many requests to be at an amazing variety of functions. Sudden emergencies arise, and one's schedule is turned topsy-turvy. The plans for the day must be reshuffled, and we forget some function we had scheduled.

Probably the main cause for a pastor's occasional absentmindedness is the constant pressure of his Sunday messages that keep rolling around in his brain. One pastor described it accurately in this way. When asked by his deacons what he did with his time, he explained that for one thing, he prepared three sermons each week that could be compared to having to prepare three college term papers every week. That sort of weekly pressure can cause us to be a bit absentminded.

So how can we keep our minds on our messages so we can build on them and improve them daily and at the same time remember to attend all of the necessary activities? The honest answer is that we probably cannot. That's where we must depend upon an assistant, a secretary, a wife, a diary or daily planner, or a combination of these.

We can easily offend individuals or groups when they are expecting us but we do not arrive. Sometimes when that occurs, their confidence in us is so shaken that there is lasting damage.

All of our appointments and engagements must be immediately recorded somewhere, either by us or by someone else on our behalf. This serves several purposes. It ensures that we have a record of our appointments. It provides a history of our activities. It keeps us from double-booking our time. It reminds us of where and when we need to be. And it allows us an opportunity to schedule study time, prayer time, R and R time, and family time. This last point is extremely important because if we don't schedule these four things ahead of time, our days will fill up, and at the end of the week we will discover we have spent no time in these crucial areas.

I have always kept my own diary. Others prefer that an assistant or secretary do it for them. Either way will work, but I would suggest that you use a diary (whether a book or a computer) that gives you hourly increments for the days of the week. Most discussions and activities can be kept to that time limit, and it keeps a few people or events from dominating your day and week.

It is also important to be able to demonstrate your work schedule as you maintain accountability relationships with your fellow elders and deacons.

There is one final, significant reason for keeping a written schedule. We live in a very litigious society, and many people are eager to sue. Pastors and churches are no longer exempt from this problem. We have become fair game. Someday you may be called on to document your whereabouts, with whom you had an appointment, and the location of that event. Careful documentation is the only safe way to provide you with a record of your activities.

SHORT-TERM ASSESSMENTS OF THE MEMBERS
SANCTIFICATION IS A SLOW PROCESS

You . . . know all about . . . my patience, love, endurance.
—2 TIMOTHY 3:10

Patience is the companion of wisdom.   —AUGUSTINE

A Christian without patience is like a soldier without arms.
—THOMAS WATSON

We've taught them plainly. We have carefully exegeted the Scriptures before them. We have illustrated our point. We have made the applications so plain that a child could understand. Our life has been a model in those particular areas. Why, then, don't they get it? Why do they keep acting that way? Didn't they listen to us? Where are their minds? What are they thinking about? A grade-school child would know better than to act in that manner. We shouldn't have to keep preaching to them over and over in this area. Maybe they are not even genuine Christians. They are sinners! That's what they are!

We're right. They are sinners. (Just like we are!) And therein lies the problem. Sin affects our nature, our thoughts, our actions, our motives, our relationships, and even our ability to listen and apply the Scriptures. Sure, a redeemed soul has the work of the Spirit in his life, and he should be expected to show definite signs of regeneration and sanctification. But the sanctifying process takes time. And it is not always a straight line in every area of our lives. Sometimes we are living in the Spirit, but other times the world, our flesh, or the devil may have the upper hand.

What we should look for is progress, not perfection. Perfection comes with our glorification, but not before. That will be the day when "we will sing and shout the victory."

So we need to understand and expect that progress is often a slow process. We can preach our hearts out and sometimes see not only very little change but even regression. That's the very reason Paul practiced patience, love, and endurance. We must also. We must never settle for spiritual mediocrity, but we must be realists. We must strive for spiritual excellence in our lives and the lives of our members but realize there will be bumpy roads and disappointments along the way. We'll fail. Our members will fail. Patience, therefore, is necessary!

☙

AVOIDING CLIQUES
WE MUST SHEPHERD THE ENTIRE FLOCK

There is no room in the church for any intellectual, spiritual or social elite which separates itself from fellow-believers whom Christ has accepted. —GEOFFREY B. WILSON

We're not all alike. We don't have the same interests. Our temperaments are different. Our backgrounds can be so diverse that it is a wonder we can be together in the same church. And yet God in His infinite wisdom calls people with many different perspectives to come together as one body in a local church.

As pastors in certain age groups with particular backgrounds, certain interests, and definite hobbies, we will have a tendency to naturally gravitate to a particular group in our church. And if we are not careful, we can easily find ourselves spending the majority of our time with them. Sure, we will attend to others' needs and problems, but when it comes time to relax and unwind with our friends, there may be a select few whom we choose.

That's the natural way to do things. But pastors don't have as much luxury in that area as laymen. We will have just a few with whom we know we can discuss deep personal matters without fear of disclosure or censure. But we must be extremely careful that we share our time and interests with as many as possible. That's part of what makes the pastor's life so demanding. There will be a variety of individuals and groups in our churches—young couples, singles, older ladies, tough-minded businessmen, and many others. And that fact calls us to stretch ourselves.

We are to be a shepherd to all of them. If any of them get the idea that we do not care about them or do not desire to be in their company, our opportunity for ministry to them comes to a halt. Oh, they may remain a part of the congregation, but their interest and enthusiasm will wane, and their service will be minimal.

The old saying that "people don't care how much we know as long as they know how much we care" is certainly true. And if our members ever develop the impression that we have joined a clique with a certain few and that we really do not care about them, our ministry with them is on its way downhill.

So how do we keep that from occurring? We must plan times to be around all sorts of people. We must cultivate a genuine interest in people of all backgrounds and involvements. Let them tell us about their work, their families, their hobbies, their fears and concerns. Visit them on their jobs and in their homes. We cannot sit around waiting for them to come to us. We must get on the phone and let them know we care and that we desire to spend time with them. Many times our own interests can be broadened, and opportunities for service that were never thought possible will indeed grow.

With a large congregation, a pastor cannot possibly give everyone equal attention nor get around to even knowing everyone. But by careful planning, group exposure to many folks can help us redeem the time and demonstrate to them that we really do care.

ᐧᕦᕧ

BEING FAIR WITH
YOUR CONGREGATION
THEY HAVE A FAMILY TO RAISE!

*No man or woman ever had a nobler challenge or a higher privilege
than to bring up a child for God and whenever we slight that privilege
or neglect that ministry for anything else, we live to mourn it in
heartache and grief.*   —VANCE HAVNER

With the advent of mega-churches have come the mega-programs in
those churches. There are multiple worship services on Sunday morning (some even on Saturday night, Friday night, and recently even on
Thursday night), Sunday evening services, Wednesday dinner and prayer
meetings, Tuesday and/or Thursday Bible classes, special seminars, outreach nights, training sessions, choir, orchestra, and drama practice,
elder and deacon meetings, committees such as long-range planning,
finance, building, hospitality, benevolence, widows, and a host of others, plus a number of other service and ministry opportunities. Then
there are softball teams, church picnics, banquets, and mission trips.

If hard-working, faithful members are not careful, pretty soon
they will find that almost every day or evening they are involved in
some committee, service, or church activity. And at the end of the
week, they are exhausted, their families have received little attention,
and necessary chores are stacking up. Bodies become tired, nerves
become frayed, and children are yelled at or ignored. God never
meant it to be that way!

Pastors love people who will be at all services and events and who
will volunteer willingly for anything that needs doing. The old adage
that 10 percent of the people do 90 percent of the work is probably
true in many congregations. And how we love that 10 percent. They
can always be counted on. But what price are they paying? Sometimes
their involvement comes at the expense of their families.

A few years ago I talked with a very prominent pastor of a large, growing church about this problem. His church's solution was that the members were not allowed to be active in more than one program. They were expected to be at the regular services, but when it came to other programs, the members had to choose between all of the options. If they sang in the choir, they were not allowed to teach Sunday school. If they served on the hospitality committee, they couldn't also lead a church-sponsored home Bible study. This church placed a high priority on families, and this was one way they showed it. Their members deserved the right to spend several nights a week with their families, and the church was not going to get in the way of that.

We must encourage and help our members have the time it takes to properly raise their families. Let's not overload them with guilt if they cannot take on another project. Rather, we should encourage them to make and keep their families their number one priority!

꙳

SETTLING THE SCORE PUBLICLY
WE'RE NOT ALLOWED TO TAKE VENGEANCE

Do not take revenge, my friends, but leave room for God's wrath, for it is written: "It is mine to avenge, I will repay," says the Lord.
—ROMANS 12:19

We've been hurt by some action or word by a member of our congregation. These things could come from a member from whom we have felt alienated. Or it could come very suddenly from someone who otherwise has been supportive of us. Either way, we are hurt and have been seething over the matter. We can't get the matter out of our minds. We lose sleep over it. It isn't fair, and we know it.

Many would strike back at least with words, perhaps even

physically. We certainly cannot do that. Yet it hurts so much that we cannot seem to let it go. As we prepare a message, the passage either directly or indirectly speaks to the issue. Aha, that's the way we will handle it. We will make a very clear point in our outline or use such an illustration that our "enemy" cannot miss it. We can speak to him in a sermon setting, and he can do nothing but sit there and take it. So we handle it in the very next sermon, and the score has been settled!

The pulpit must never be used for bashing our enemies or anyone in our congregation.

But has it? We have probably not only further angered the person and his confidants, but we have clearly violated a number of passages of Scripture (Romans 12:19 for sure, along with Matthew 18:15-18). Vengeance is the Lord's and His only. And Matthew 18 gives us clear directions as to how to deal with a brother who has sinned against us. Further, 1 Corinthians 13 tells us to bear all things. Was this a matter we should have borne? What sort of example have we set? The pulpit must never be used for bashing our enemies or anyone in our congregation.

The church is God's flock for which Christ died. We must always nurture and care for it. We must never, never act in a manner that would harm it.

The Word of God is very clear that there are private ways of dealing with personal sins. If those private methods do not resolve the matter, Matthew 18 provides the next steps, which ultimately might involve public disclosure, but only after all of the earlier appropriate steps have been followed. We are the spiritual leaders. Therefore we must set the appropriate example in dealing with people, especially with those whom we think have wronged us.

⌐🐗

LOOKING DOWN ON OTHERS

THE ONLY REASON WE ARE HIGHER UP IS THAT WE ARE STANDING ON A THREE-FOOT PLATFORM

No man who is full of himself can ever truly preach the Christ who emptied himself.   —J. SIDLOW BAXTER

There are a lot of temptations for pastors, one of which, because of our public role, is to think of ourselves more highly than we should. And in so doing, we can develop a tendency to depreciate those who are under our leadership.

This can be manifested in a number of ways. Our messages can be occasions where we talk down to people. We can berate people about particular sins, though our own sins are just as heinous. We can assume a know-it-all attitude. We can conduct meetings in such a way that we take advantage of people or make light of their thoughts or suggestions. We can make public, veiled references to people. And we can use humor about our members from the pulpit at their emotional expense.

There are several antidotes that should help keep us from such an attitude or action. First, grasping a realistic view of our sinfulness and weaknesses should truly produce a humble spirit. We are corrupt, and apart from the grace of God we genuinely deserve God's wrath.

Second, realizing that anything that has been accomplished in our ministry has been solely the result of God's wonderful grace also humbles us. The truth is, we do not have the ability to even move a feather spiritually. The sovereign Spirit of God is the sole life-giving and life-changing Person.

And third, the only reason we are even allowed the awesome opportunity to have a ministry is that God has put us there. I'm reminded of an often used illustration. It seems a man was walking through a field and came to a barbed-wire fence and on top of a fence post sat a turtle. It was obvious that the turtle did not make it to the top of that post by himself. Someone had to have put him there. In the same way, no minister of the Gospel should have the audacity to think he has by his own abilities risen to any level. God is the only One who can give us a genuinely effective ministry.

If these wholesome realities are constantly kept in mind, our attitudes toward those to whom we minister will be characterized by humility, gratitude, kindness, and patience. Otherwise we are unfit for the gospel ministry.

♦

"I'LL PRAY FOR YOU"
DO NOT PROMISE IT UNLESS YOU MEAN IT

One of the gravest perils which besets the ministry is a restless scattering of energies over an amazing multiplicity of interests which leaves no margin of time and of strength for receptive and absorbing communion with God. —ANDREW BONAR

If you've been in the ministry for any time at all, you've been asked by numerous people to pray for them. Those requests come with a variety of subjects. We are asked to pray for someone's salvation, for sick people, for marriages, for personal and family relationships, for job searches, for relocation plans, for financial conditions, for proper attitudes toward people and events, for children, for people in sin, for travel plans, and for many other things absolutely too numerous to mention.

In one humorous story a woman called a Baptist pastor to ask him to pray for her dog. The pastor explained that he had never before been asked to pray for a dog. The woman explained that she had planned to make a large donation to his church in honor of her dog. The pastor immediately replied, "Oh, I'm sorry—I didn't realize he was a Baptist dog." Certainly he would pray for her dog!

We get so many requests to pray for people that it is very easy to promise to do so and then forget what we have promised. And that is wrong. Our yes must be yes, and our no must be no. We must be men of our word. If we have told someone we will pray for his or her requests, we must do so.

We have few alternatives. We can say, "No, I cannot in conscience pray for that." Or we can promise to do so and then do it. But we must not say we will, then forget about it.

A very good practice for us is, when possible, to stop right then and there and pray for the request in the person's presence. If it is a request that comes to us through the telephone, we can pray with them over the phone. If the request comes in a public setting we can, in good taste, pray then also. In either event, that will let them know we take their requests seriously. It may also help us to remember to pray about the matters at a later date.

It would be good for us as pastors to have a prayer diary in which we can record all the legitimate needs we plan to carry before our God. Then daily we can fulfill those promises.

We must be men of the Word, men of prayer, and men of our word. We must never promise our members anything that we do not have a full intention of fulfilling.

***

LISTENING TO COMPLAINTS
CONSIDER WHAT THEY ARE SAYING, BUT DON'T LET IT GET YOU DOWN

He who heeds discipline shows the way of life, but whoever ignores correction leads others astray. —PROVERBS 10:17

Complaints! They are part of the church scene. They will come in all shapes, sizes, and intensity.

Some will come from those who are often unhappy and simply have a complaining spirit. Others will present complaints regarding matters about which they have little information and that they have not thought through to any degree. Others will be attempting to help us in our walk, teaching, administration, or leadership. Some will be good suggestions and should not be considered complaints. These should be welcomed and used beneficially. Some will come with hostile attitudes, and others will be brought to us with a very gentle spirit. But they will come, and we might as well be ready for them. They are a fact of church life, because a church is simply a group of called-out people who rightly feel some form of ownership. Some love the church deeply and genuinely want to help. Others have been offended and are simply striking out. In either case, they do deserve our attention, but never should they leave us depressed.

A church is simply a group of called-out people who rightly feel some form of ownership.

How should we handle such situations? First, we need to listen very carefully to learn what is being said. We should ask questions and repeat the person's complaint to him or her to make sure we understand it. Are there clear scriptural principles involved? If possible and needed, we could talk it over with our fellow elders/pastors so they can help us think through the matter. Often we should not try to carry the whole load ourselves, for there is wisdom in many godly counselors. Though it is difficult not to, we must try our best to avoid taking personal offense, using the occasion as an opportunity to either grow ourselves or to help the complainer grow in Christlikeness.

The apostle Paul felt the jealousy and complaints of his fellow pastors in Rome while in prison, but rather than striking out or becoming depressed, he simply rejoiced that the Gospel was being preached. We, too, can often turn a complaint into something positive.

Recalling our Lord's humbly washing the dirty, smelly feet of His disciples should remind us that we are called to be servants. That should be our focus rather than the negative comments of those who come to us with complaints.

MEMBERS WITH VAGUE COMPLAINTS
THEY'RE NEVER SATISFIED

Do everything without complaining. —PHILIPPIANS 2:14

These men are grumblers and faultfinders. —JUDE 16

At some point we will all face them. They are the ones who really try our patience and often cause us to seriously question our call. Their concerns are seldom expressed in a constructive manner, and rarely do they offer better ways of doing things. They only know that things are not the way things ought to be in the church.

You work hard to understand their point, but often it is elusive. You cannot quite figure out why they look at the same sermons or actions or programs and come up with an altogether different attitude about them than the other members. At times you wish they would get it all out once and for all and get it over with, but that's not their style. They are always just mildly negative, but not enough for church discipline; otherwise you would know clearly how to handle them.

When they talk to you, often their words are something like this: "I just don't know, but I don't feel good about such and such." Or "Pastor, I just don't feel we're making progress." Or "Something just doesn't seem right." They really vex you, and when you see them heading for your office, you cringe or want to slip out the back door unseen.

What are we to do? Sometimes there is not much we can do, except to limit our time around them. We have other more positive members who think clearly and can tell us distinctly just what they agree with and what they do not agree with.

But we *can* do some things. First, notice the words they are using: "I don't *feel*," or "something just doesn't *seem* right." That tells us that what they are experiencing is very subjective and cannot really be dealt with until it can be brought into objective analysis. And, second, we can tell them that they must be able to articulate clearly what it is they are upset about. There is no way we can deal with their concerns unless they can provide us with clear information, provide some possible solutions, and make a specific recommendation to solve the problem. Otherwise, our time, energy, and emotions can be used up in a fruitless search for answers to very nebulous issues.

These people are members of our flock and do have the right to come to us. But we also have the responsibility as shepherds to help them learn how to approach matters biblically.

GETTING THE FACTS
WE MUST NOT JUMP TOO QUICKLY TO A CONCLUSION

The first to present his case seems right, till another comes forward and questions him. —PROVERBS 18:17

There are going to be disputes in our churches. Members are going to disagree with each other from time to time. A church is made up of sinners, saved sinners at best, but nevertheless sinners who from time to time will live in the flesh. At times these matters escalate into very serious problems, threatening the peace of the church and even at times causing a serious split in the body. People line up to take sides.

Occasionally it is all one-sided and there clearly is a right and a wrong. But most often there are three sides — Richard's side, Henry's side, and God's side. We want to be on God's side. Therein lies the solution, but it takes time to sort through matters. We must realize that just because we have been called to the ministry does not mean we have the ability to automatically know where the truth is. That will take time, effort, patience, and much prayer.

First, we must make sure that we gather all the pertinent facts. We must not jump to conclusions, especially if we are closer to one member than the other. If we are, our emotions may affect our judgment and cause us to cloud the issues. We should interview both members and also others involved in the problem. Next we should soak everything in fervent prayer, asking God for wisdom in these matters. At this level we must keep the matters as confidential as possible, though there are times when it will be necessary and helpful to involve the godly wisdom of other church leaders, providing that will not compromise confidentiality. We should make certain that we know the biblical principles that apply to the matters before us.

A church is made up of sinners, saved sinners at best, but nevertheless sinners.

We must make it abundantly plain which issues are addressed by the Word of God and those issues on which we can simply give our personal opinion. Call on all involved to live with such unity passages as Philippians 2:1-18 and 4:2-9. It is helpful to give the parties specific assignments that force them to think biblically about how to resolve the issues. Encourage them to pray together that God would help them solve these matters. Spend time with them, teaching them how Satan would love to sow division in the body of Christ.

Lastly, if there is a one-sided issue and the guilty party refuses to make peace, we must not hesitate to follow Christ's instructions in Matthew 18:15-18. That may be distasteful and hard to carry out, but God always knows best!

ᕯ

OPEN REBUKE
IT REQUIRES US TO BE COURAGEOUS

Better is open rebuke than hidden love. The kisses of an enemy may be profuse, but faithful are the wounds of a friend.
—PROVERBS 27:5-6

The book of Proverbs lets us know that rebuke is good, needed, and commanded. As pastors, we are commanded to rebuke those who need it and to not let them disregard us (1 Tim. 4:11-16 and 2 Tim. 3:16-17).

But it is easy to gossip to others about the weaknesses and failures of certain individuals rather than going to the persons themselves. When we do this, we violate many clear principles of Scripture. We are told to go to the individual. We are told to go to him privately. We are told to forgive him if he repents. If not, we are next to take private witnesses. If there is no repentance, step 3 is to bring the matter to the church; and if there is still no repentance after the church addresses the issue, the church must formally disfellowship the member. But unfortunately, rarely is this process carried out. Instead, there is too much gossip and backbiting in God's church.

We pastors are not immune to these sins. It is hard to confront people directly. I'm sure Nathan's knees were knocking when he told King David, "You are the man!" But he did confront David, and eventually great good came from that confrontation. Sure, David, his family, and his kingdom suffered greatly. But David himself informs us that the joy of his salvation returned, and his psalms testify of a repentant king.

Rebuke must be administered carefully and only after we have gathered sufficient, irrefutable evidence of an unrepentant attitude. If it is a matter of their ignorance of biblical attitudes or morality, our rebuke must be in the form of gentle instruction. But if it is a matter of a high disregard of God's standards (and not our own personal ones), our rebuke must be firm and clear. Even then patience must be exercised, allowing the Spirit of God to work in their hearts. But given a reasonable period of time, the rebuke may need to be coupled with a command to forsake that sin immediately.

That's tough love. It takes courage. But more than that, it requires believing that God's Word and His principles work, and that "better is open rebuke than hidden love"!

༆

FEAR OF THE CONGREGATION
THOUGH THE TRUTH MAY SOMETIMES HURT, IT MUST ALWAYS BE TOLD (IN LOVE)

Kings take pleasure in honest lips; they value a man who speaks the truth.
—PROVERBS 16:13

If "kings take pleasure in honest lips," imagine how much the great King of this universe must be pleased when we speak the truth. And since the church is His institution, and since He gave His only Son for the church, imagine how pleased He must be when we speak the truth to His people.

The Bible is not a book that teaches us "how to win friends and influence people," if by that we mean that we hold back the truth and do not give people what they need to hear for fear of offending them. In fact, it is a book that teaches us to do the opposite. Sometimes the truth hurts, but the truth will set men free.

It is no fun to be disliked. We enjoy being held in high regard by people. We want them to feel comfortable around us and to not be put off by our clerical trappings and persona. It is right that our lives not cause an offense and that our attitudes, walk, and personality attract people rather than drive them away. But we must be prepared for our message to sometimes cause a separation.

If we ever get to the point where our message is rounded off so that we avoid a particular passage, a needed subject, a pointed rebuke or biblical command for fear that we are going to offend and thereby run off a member, then we have begun to fear men rather than striving to please our Master.

That's a temptation into which Satan wants us to fall. He wants people leaving after our messages very comfortable, soothed, and feeling good about us. But sometimes, in order for us to be faithful, some people will leave the message not feeling very good about us. The truth should comfort the hurting but also unsettle the comfortable.

Our eyes should never be on the size of our church, the success of our programs, our budget, our salaries, but on speaking the truth of our Lord. Our concern must be the repentance, salvation, and spiritual growth of our hearers. To fear men is to hold God's Word up for contempt; to fear God is to speak His message truthfully and faithfully.

ᵔᵔ

LETTING CHURCH PROBLEMS FESTER
WE'RE ABOUT TO SEE IT EXPLODE

I plead with Euodia and I plead with Syntyche to agree with each other in the Lord. Yes, and I ask you, local yokefellow, help these women who have contended at my side in the cause of the gospel.
—PHILIPPIANS 4:2-3A

Time heals things. We've heard that many times. And occasionally it is true that people's emotions die down and they lose the heart to disagree or fight. But to depend on time alone in the body of Christ to mend church problems is a very dangerous path. More often than not the problems only fester, become more serious, and then explode.

Christ calls His body to peace. Pastors are to be chief peacemakers. Simply looking away from a problem offers bad leadership and puts our congregation in great peril. What often starts as a small matter can quickly escalate into a major struggle.

If a brother sins against another, Christ tells us how to handle that (Matthew 18:15-18). If something is defective in the church, Paul tells us to correct it (1 Thess. 5:12-24). When a false teacher arose in the body, Paul quickly responded to the heresy (Gal. 1:6-10). Even when

Peter's actions were clouding the Gospel, Paul got right to the point, opposing Peter to his face (Gal. 2:14).

Satan is happy when problems occur in the body of Christ. He loves divisions, dissensions, uproars, individual against individual, falsehood against truth, lies, distortions, and other things that upset the tranquillity and mission of the church. And one of his insidious ways of fostering these problems is to cause the leadership to assume that we just need to give the matter a bit of time to see if it won't work itself out. Seldom is that the case! Some very minor issues are best left alone, but when they escalate to major issues, time will work against us rather than for us. We must not fall into Satan's trap. He is for real!

CHURCH HOPPING BY THE MEMBERS
IT IS A CONSTANT REALITY!

I believe that one reason why the church of God at this present moment has so little influence over the world is because the world has so much influence over the church. —C. H. SPURGEON

Be united with other Christians. A wall with loose bricks is not good. The bricks must be cemented together. —CORRIE TEN BOOM

It can really hurt when you lose members to other congregations within your locality. Often these will be people who have supported you, served faithfully with you, and were the ones to whom you turned for encouragement.

Then, without warning, you find that they are leaving. It can be devastating to your morale. And on top of that, their leaving and the resulting talk can stir up others who also eventually leave.

Though sometimes those going elsewhere clearly have guidance from the Lord, at other times that does not seem to be the case. You neither understand nor agree with their leaving. You talk with them, plead with them to stay, but in the end they leave anyway. There is nothing you can say or do that will persuade them to stay. You fear that their exit might trigger a stampede of others also. You want to go to sleep and wake up from this bad dream. But the reality is still with you. You fret about it and become discouraged. It takes a long time to overcome the disappointment.

This is going to happen to us, so we need to be prepared for it. In many ways we can do nothing about these situations. We can try harder to prevent it, but the inevitable will surely occur.

There are several things, however, that we can do ahead of time. One: we must teach those in our congregation what is involved in becoming members. They are actually becoming a part of a family. And family members seldom leave a family. There are mutual, long-range responsibilities and privileges that must be recognized and honored. Just because a new family appears that might initially be a bit more attractive does not mean you should divorce your old family and move to the new one.

Two: we need to teach them what love is. Love is action and involves seeking the highest good for others. Often when people leave a congregation, it is because of their desire to get something better for themselves, rather than staying the course so they can serve others.

People jump to new congregations because of the perceived excitement there. There is something inherently dynamic about a new, faster-growing body. We see this often in the new movement known as the "seeker-sensitive" churches that are springing up all around us. So three: Without harming a genuine movement of the Spirit of God, we need to educate our members on what God accepts as worship and what He approves regarding long-term commitments.

Despite all of this, we will still experience loss of members to other bodies. When we do, we can wish them well, seek to maintain some contact with them, and pray for them. If they are genuine believers, God is still their Savior, and they are still our brothers and sisters in Christ. In fact, the Christian family is the church at large—the universal body of Christ. When our members move to another local body, they are still a part of the family. Perhaps in God's providence He is simply rearranging the kingdom for purposes yet to be made known to us. We must trust Him in these times.

When the Lord appears and calls us all home, we will all be back together worshiping the Lamb of God for eternity, all together around the one throne. There may be separate bodies now, but a time will come when there is but one great body.

When people do leave our church, we as leaders should also take a hard look at ourselves to see if we are part of the reason for the exodus. Such continuous self-evaluation of our leadership, teaching, shepherding, and programs might reveal to us that the fault lies with us rather than with those who are moving to other congregations. For this reason, exit interviews can be very helpful, especially if we hope to correct deficiencies that are brought to light.

PEOPLE WHO ARE RELOCATED
IT IS GOING TO HAPPEN, AND IT HURTS

Nothing less than a living sacrifice is demanded. Not a loan, but a gift; not a compromise, but a sacrifice; not our poorest, but our best. Not a dead but a living offering. Each drop of our blood, each ounce of our energy, each throb of our heart, we must offer to God.

—JOSEPH PEARCE

I never made a sacrifice. We ought not to talk of sacrifice when we remember the great sacrifice that he made who left his Father's throne on high to give himself for us. —DAVID LIVINGSTONE

If you have been in the ministry for a while, you have experienced a profound hurt caused by something about which you could do nothing. If you have not yet experienced the following, just wait—it will occur.

You are going to receive a call from one of your very best members, one whom you have poured your life into, someone whom you have counted as one of the closest friends you have in the church. And he is going to want to take you to lunch to give you some news. You speculate all day but cannot imagine what the news is. At lunch you are stunned when he removes the mystery. His company is transferring him next month to another state. He has already signed a contract on his home, and the move is certain.

Suddenly your world is turned upside-down. You think of the hundreds of hours you have spent with this family. You think of the crises through which you have helped them work. You are reminded of the many times both families have shared baby-sitting. You remember how the children grew up together and the games and picnics you enjoyed together. Your wife and his wife are best friends, and you know what that loss is going to mean to them. You remember when he became a deacon, then later when he was put forward as an elder. The congregation unanimously voted him into the office. You remember how he spent several entire nights encouraging you when things were rough at the church. He hardly got to bed those nights, but he never complained. He was the one who helped keep you going.

God sometimes works in mysterious ways His wonders to perform. And maybe the thing He plans to perform is to strengthen this family somehow through the move, and perhaps even to extend the Gospel to a new locality.

So your heart is breaking. You want to rejoice at his well-deserved promotion, but there is an empty feeling in the pit of your stomach. You wish him well, tell him how much you will miss him, then on the way back to the office you break down in the car.

He and his family have been closer to you than many of your own blood relatives. You feel what the Ephesian elders must have felt (in Acts 20) when Paul told them good-bye and they wept.

If that has not yet occurred in your ministry, just hang on—it will. When it does, how should you react? What is the godly way of handling such a huge disappointment?

Our reactions should take different paths, depending upon the particular circumstances. First, we must make certain that the person or family is not running away from problems, obligations, or spiritual responsibilities. And we need to know the spiritual climate they are moving into. Is there a solid evangelical church where they can be fed and can serve? If not, do they plan to start a faithful work of the Lord in that area? Will his new job responsibilities interfere with the time he needs for his family and his spiritual obligations? Will his job put him into any unusually tempting situations? Does he plan to use his big raise to further support the work of the Gospel? Is his wife solidly in favor of this move? Have they prayed earnestly for direction? Are they violating Scriptures in any way by this move? Do they really think this move will be spiritually good for the family?

It is difficult for those who are left behind in this situation to rejoice. But perhaps in God's providence all of the ministry to this family has occurred so that what they have learned is now going to be shared in another part of God's vineyard. Or perhaps God is putting those family members to a test to prove their faith or to prove that their commitment to service is genuine. Or there could be things they need to learn from other ministries to round out their Christian experience.

God sometimes works in mysterious ways His wonders to perform. And maybe the thing He plans to perform is to strengthen this family somehow through the move, and perhaps even to extend the Gospel to a new locality. At this point we must trust Him, even through tears. He knows what He is doing. And He is trustworthy. But it still hurts!

❧

CHANGING YOUR CHURCH
GRANTED, THE CHURCH MAY
NEED SOME CHANGES, BUT LET'S NOT
TEAR IT UP IN THE PROCESS

I believe that in public worship we should do well to be bound by no human rules, and constrained by no stereotyped order.
—CHARLES H. SPURGEON

Anything which makes it easier for us to worship spiritually should be encouraged while anything that draws attention to itself rather than to God should be eliminated from our corporate services.
—ROBERT G. RAYBURN

It has been said that eventually a church will reflect the personality of its pastor. Pastors will invariably institute significant changes in the churches in which they are called to serve. For example, young men just graduating from seminaries may come to a church with "fresh, innovative ideas." Or a pastor is brought from another congregation and brings with him ways in which ministry was conducted in his previous pastorate. Or an existing pastor may have discovered biblical truth that has not been known or preached before in that congregation. Or he may come back from a conference or seminar full of new ideas that he hopes will "revolutionize" his church.

Many of these new concepts will be good, practical, needed, and readily accepted by the congregation. Instituting them will create no serious problems. But some changes will meet with stiff resistance, and when suddenly thrust upon the church they can damage the unity of the body and can at times be the occasion of a church split.

How do we know when and how to push for needed changes? How much time should we allow for members to think about, question, and accept change? What areas should we live with, knowing full well that they should be changed to enable the church to become more effective or efficient? To know all of the answers to these questions would require the wisdom of Solomon. But here are some thoughts that might be helpful.

- If the area involves the basics of the Gospel (such as the depravity of man, the substitutionary atonement of Christ, salvation by grace though faith alone, the bodily resurrection and imminent return of Christ, the inspiration and authority of the Scriptures), we have no alternative but to begin immediately teaching and preaching on these areas. We must seek change at once. The basic Christian message is at stake.
- If the area involves general biblical truth (such as the mode of baptism, Christian liberty, the sovereignty of God, or financial stewardship), we should seek to first teach the leadership and then the congregation, but must do so very patiently. Though each one of these areas is important, we should be careful that we do not ram these positions down people's throats. Long-held traditions and beliefs require time to rethink. We can do great damage by advancing like a bull in a china shop, insisting upon immediate response. By patiently teaching the leadership, and then the members, what the Word of God actually says in these areas, we give the Spirit of God opportunity to work in their lives to enable them to digest biblical truth. "A man convinced against his will is of the same opinion still," but those members taught by the Spirit of God will indeed be changed.
- If the matters do not involve biblical truth but rather personal preferences, we must introduce changes very carefully and patiently. Examples could be the particular type of Sunday school, the type of worship service, the order of service, or a move to a new location. Here also we must work through the established leadership and seek to gain a unanimity, or at least a consensus; if such agreement is not reached, we should think about giving up our plans. The leadership then must patiently lead the congregation, giving time for the flock to ask questions and make suggestions. No immediate action is generally

needed. Time for the congregation to give input and to gradually become comfortable with the idea of doing things differently can often reap good results.

• When there is a change needed that is going to seriously affect people's lives and also requires church action heretofore never done, a prolonged teaching program must be instituted. Two examples here could be: (1) when a new form of elder rule and shepherding program is begun; (2) when a formal biblical church-discipline program is instituted. These are significant issues and can cause fractures within the church body when the congregation is forced to change immediately. These matters can involve long-standing traditions. When members are pressed in these areas, they may react emotionally. Patient teaching and exemplary leadership can be the key to effectively instituting changes in such areas.

An immature or impatient pastor can do great harm to the unity of the body. He must learn to listen to the collective wisdom of his own staff, the members, and other established pastors on whether, when, and how to change a church. Destroying a church in the process is definitely not the answer.

⌒☜

LEAVING A CHURCH
MINISTRY IS A LONG-HAUL BUSINESS

A preacher should have the mind of a scholar, the heart of a child and the hide of a rhinoceros. His biggest problem is how to toughen his hide without hardening his heart.   —VANCE HAVNER

Disappointments in the ministry come regularly. Problems and disagreements among the congregation and among church leaders are common. The ministry deals with people, and at times people can be very trying. The hours are irregular and often long. The deadlines are weekly, sometimes daily. At times there is more criticism of the pastor than praise, prayer, or help for him. Some of the problems he must face are very complex, and the wisdom of Solomon is needed and sorely desired, but often not forthcoming. Fear of public failure is always present. And so it is no wonder we occasionally think of quitting, leaving the church, moving away, or taking a secular job.

It does not surprise me that the majority of pastors harbor those thoughts at some point, perhaps several times, in their ministry. During those distressing days, Paul's words in 2 Timothy 4:7 are so very convicting and encouraging: "I have fought the good fight, I have finished the race, I have kept the faith." We all know that the great apostle kept going despite many more persecutions, deprivations, and church problems than we will probably ever face. And he said that on top of all of the matters he faced, there was the constant concern on his part for "all the churches" (2 Cor. 11:28).

His grace seems to be especially poured out on those who stay the course

---

"All the churches"! We usually have only one church to look after. Paul had many, and he knew intimately about most of the false teachings they faced, the sins in which they were living, the hopelessness and despair they were suffering, the hostility toward him in some of them, and their need for godly, mature leadership. That's enough to overwhelm or discourage any man!

Yet there he was, at the very end of his life, with many of his helpers having forsaken him, still fighting the good fight, finishing the race, and keeping the faith. We say, "What a valiant soldier for Christ." And we stand in wonder and amazement at this great man.

Our own problems at times seem insurmountable, and no solutions appear in sight. But we can't see as far down the road as God can. His grace seems to be especially poured out on those who stay the course. Though the world, and sometimes even the church world, seems chaotic, God has His hand on all people, events, movements, and attitudes. He is sovereign. He is in charge. We simply must stay the course and trust Him. Things that at times appear to have no workable solution are often surprisingly resolved in ways we would never have imagined.

The ministry is not for the timid. It is not for those who run from problems. It is not for quitters. It is a long-haul business!

STEPPING DOWN
WE CAN STAY TOO LONG

I have never yet known the Spirit of God to work where the Lord's people were divided. —D. L. MOODY

One of the most successful evangelical pastors in our area stayed too long at his church. He was a leader among the pastors in our locality. His church was respected. He was deeply loved by his own congregation and by his peers as he led the fight to keep liberalism from encroaching into our churches. His church was thriving and was worshiping in a new, expanded facility. The area in which his ministry was located continued to grow dramatically. Everything seemed just right, and it was expected that when he turned the reins over to a successor an ongoing, dynamic ministry would continue.

But he would not step down. His age advanced well beyond normal retirement. His health began to fade. His sermons began to lose their appeal. His influence began to wane. The members and even some of the leadership began to move elsewhere. Young couples began moving their memberships to other churches. Only his close, personal friends stayed with him, many of whom were quite old and less mobile, hence not very energetic when it came to the work of the Gospel.

As he saw his ministry begin to fade, he became bitter and very caustic. Squabbles erupted within the remaining members. Eventually the church voted to vacate the pulpit. Things became very acrimonious. The pastor left the ministry as a tired, pitiful, bitter old man.

Yet he could not blame others. It was painfully evident years earlier that he should have planned for a successor. Why he did not, I fail to understand. I was asked to fill his pulpit on several occasions, and what was beginning to take place was painfully clear.

Continuing beyond our effectiveness can happen to any of us. There is definitely something positive to be said of those pastors who do not jump from church to church but stay the course as they shepherd the sheep through thick and thin. But there comes a time when we must begin the plans to step down and turn our ministry over to a successor.

We may not always know when that proper time is. It will be a different time for each of us, depending on a number of variables. But we should have sufficient leadership around us who will be open and honest and will help us recognize the optimum time for the welfare of the flock.

It is admirable for men to be willing to stay on until the Lord calls them home. But sometimes that may not be in the best interest of the flock.

LEAVING A LEGACY
WHEN WE'RE GONE, WILL THE WORK SURVIVE?

And the things you have heard me say in the presence of many witnesses entrust to reliable men who will also be qualified to teach others.
—2 TIMOTHY 2:2

Whether you are there yet or not, someday this will be your situation: You've worked very hard for many years to build a congregation of godly people. You know that God is the one who has done it through you, and you take no credit for the spiritual successes. You are jealous for the welfare of your members. You want to protect them from false teachings and destructive influences. You know that you basically understand God's truth and that your instructions to your members have been solidly biblical, and that they have responded marvelously. As their shepherd, you will guard them until God removes you from the scene.

Furthermore, you have basically been alone. It has been you (the shepherd) and the members (the sheep). From time to time you have given some of the members opportunity for teaching, preaching, or leadership, but it has been subpar, and you have been burned by their mistakes. You don't want those mistakes perpetuated in the church; so you are the only one up front week by week.

But then, with little advance notice, God decides to take you home. The people are left with no leadership. The only thing left for them is to form a pulpit committee and begin the arduous search for a new pastor. Sometimes that takes months, even years, and the church suffers during the interim. The interim preachers can do very little other than preach. They cannot provide the full-orbed shepherding that is needed, simply because they are temporary, often part-time, and the church views them as such.

Finally a new pastor is selected, but it takes a long time to really know a person. Because the new pastor does not yet know the flock and the congregation has not yet gotten comfortable with him, little shepherding can take place immediately. In that situation the church may begin to crumble.

What causes all of this chaos? Violating 1 Timothy 2:2. All Christians should constantly be training others to carry on the work of the Gospel. This is especially true with pastors. We must recognize our frailties and mortality and always be about the work of discipling others, preparing them for leadership roles. We are in the process of departing the scene. We must be prepared to transfer the mantle to other capable men. Paul did. He transferred it to Timothy (and others), and he told Timothy to transfer it to others who could transfer it yet again.

CHURCH HOPPING BY THE PASTOR
IT IS A CURSE!

He who would be a faithful minister of the gospel must deny the pride of his heart, be emptied of ambition, and set himself wholly to seek the glory of God in his calling. —WILLIAM PERKINS

As I grew up in a small denominational church, I was accustomed to frequent pastoral changes. Occasionally it was because the deacons and members thought things were not going well and a new pastor might provide the needed changes. So a vote would be taken to vacate the pulpit, and a search committee would be formed to locate "a new man of God."

But there were other times when the pastor felt he was "called of God" to relocate to a new church. Usually it was to a larger, more prominent congregation within our denomination. He had "prayed about the matter and felt God's leading to move on."

The combination of these two methods of change occurred so frequently that the name of only one of the pastors who preached to me in those early years sticks in my memory. It seems that there were so many changes, I hardly got to know any of them. Our family did move a number of times, but mostly in the same city, and I usually attended the same church.

Now, there is nothing in the Word of God that specifically states we cannot relocate to another pastorate. And I have no intention of trying to straitjacket the genuine leading of the Spirit of God, who may from time to time move a pastor to another body. However, I would say that the biblical norm is a pastor staying with his flock for a long period of time. Though the churches in the New Testament were all new, and there apparently was only one church in each location, there is no example of a pastor moving to another church. It appears that the only men moving from one church to another were the evangelists and apostles (along with their traveling companions).

It takes years to really get to know a flock and to know how to shepherd each individual. Moving every few years severely restricts our ability to pastor a flock of God's people in the way that He dictates. And we are not only to be their shepherd but also to serve as their example. Just a few years with them does not provide sufficient time for the congregation to see us serve as an example in many different situations.

One of the curses of the ministry is that pastors church-hop for larger congregations and larger salaries. Recently the pastor of a well-known church left to go to a much larger church in a larger city. Before accepting the call to a specific church, he was contacted by another church in that same vicinity. Rather than moving purely from a ministry perspective he let the two churches get into a financial bidding war. Each church kept moving its salary package higher and higher. When one of them stopped, saying they had reached the maximum they could pay, the other congregation topped that amount. It was then that the pastor said he "felt called of God" to move to that particular congregation. The salary package escalated to a point that it rivaled the salary paid by some of the larger corporations to their top executives. I couldn't help wondering just what our Lord thought about that sort of decision. I wonder if He wasn't both grieved and thoroughly disgusted.

Sometimes a pastor's ministry to a particular church does come to an end and change is better for both, but the decision should be a joint one. The entire church leadership should be involved, and if that occurs, there should be no acrimony. It should be prayed over at length, explored in every detail, and handled in an open and aboveboard manner. Both parties should genuinely agree that this is the best plan for God's Kingdom. When that is done, I believe we can expect God to bless those changes. But to continually hire and fire pastors, and for pastors to church-hop must be displeasing to the Lord and is very disruptive to the congregations.

FOR ADDITIONAL STUDY

The Church and Church Life

Originated in the mind of God: Ephesians 3:10.

Permanence and invincibility: Matthew 16:16-18.

Inhabited by God Himself: Hebrews 12:23.

Christ the head: Ephesians 1:22-23; 5:23.

Bought by Christ's blood: Acts 20:28.

The bride of Christ: Ephesians 5:25-32; Revelation 19:7.

Relationship to Christ: John 15:1-17.

Began at Pentecost: Acts 2:1-47.

Hated by the world: John 15:18-25.

Sacrifice for each other: Acts 4:33-35.

Persecuted: Acts 12:1-19.

Grows through Paul's ministry: Acts 13—28.

Leadership, teaching, protection: Acts 20:17-38; 1 Corinthians 1:20—4:21; 2 Corinthians 10:1—13:10; Galatians 1:6—5:12; Ephesians 4:11-16; 1 Thessalonians 2:1—3:11; 1 Timothy; 2 Timothy; Titus 1:5—2:15; Hebrews 13:7, 17.

Church discipline: Matthew 18:15-18; Acts 5:1-11; 1 Corinthians 5:1—6:11; 2 Corinthians 2:5-11; 1 Thessalonians 5:11-15; 2 Thessalonians 3:6-15; 1 Timothy 5:19-21.

Problems in the church: Acts 5:1-11; 6:1-7; 15:1-35; Romans 14:1—15:13; 1 Corinthians 5:1—6:11; 1 Corinthians 8:1-13; 10—11; Gal. 1:6-10; 3:1-5; Philippians 4:2-3; 2 Thessalonians 3:11-15; Jude 3-16.

Gifts in the church: Romans 12; 1 Corinthians 12—14; Ephesians 4:1-16; 1 Peter 4:7-11.

Raptured: 1 Corinthians 15; 1 Thessalonians 4:13—5:11.

Section Six

COUNSELING

PASTORAL COUNSELING
BY GOD'S GRACE AND WORD,
WE CAN HELP PEOPLE

I myself am convinced, my brothers, that you yourselves are full of goodness, complete in knowledge and competent to instruct one another. —ROMANS 15:14

His divine power has given us everything we need for life and godliness through our knowledge of him who has called us by his own glory and goodness. —2 PETER 1:3

In these brief comments we will not even scratch the surface on the subject of pastoral counseling. Dr. Jay Adams has done pioneering work in this area to recover the whole practice of pastors who counsel and is considered the father of "Nouthetic Counseling" (taken from the Greek word *noutheteo* found in Romans 15:14, quoted above). His many writings, beginning with his ground-breaking book *Competent to Counsel*, should all be purchased and studied carefully. For years he edited the helpful series "Journal of Pastoral Practice" (later entitled "Journal of Biblical Counseling," now edited by David Powlison), which makes an important contribution to this whole area.

From Dr. Adams's work has emerged the National Association of Nouthetic Counselors (NANC), which meets annually to further this ever-enlarging movement. The speakers and participants at these meetings, along with the books they recommend, can be genuinely helpful to pastors, especially to those who carry an increasing load of counseling. NANC certifies counselors after completion of their prescribed program of study and supervised counseling sessions. NANC also will provide pastors with lists of certified counselors in any geographical area.

The problems that affect modern man call on every bit of skill, knowledge, wisdom, and patience we can muster. Problems we deal with include serious marriage issues, parent-child difficulties, job-related problems, depression, extreme jealousy and selfishness, financial irresponsibility, spiritual laziness, tyrannical moods, unsubmissiveness, patterns of dishonesty, sexual molestation, bizarre behavior, alcohol and drug addictions, and even murder.

We will be called on to help people who have been labeled hyperactive, manic-depressive (bipolar), codependent, obsessive-compulsive, alcoholic, schizophrenic, and those with attention deficit disorder. Many of these will be people who have experienced serious, prolonged emotional and physical problems. They may have been given all sorts of conflicting advice and different forms of mind-altering and mood-altering drugs. Some of them may have spent time in institutions under the care of therapists and psychiatrists and in some instances may even have had physical operations designed to correct their problems.

By the time some of these people come to us, their lives are in complete shambles. Their families are worn out, and they have almost lost hope. Often the individuals are so hopeless and negative, and so medicated, that the pastor is faced with the serious problem of just trying to establish basic communication. We are there to help, however, and so we must begin.

Where do we begin? There are some basic things that we must somehow get across to these people in trouble.

- They must be brought face to face with the reality and true nature of sin. All of their problems can be traced back to sin—Adam's representative sin in the garden that can account for mankind's problems: personal sin, illness, bizarre behavior, death, and all other forms of suffering. Because of Adam's sin, men are born into this world with a sinful nature that gets them into all sorts of trouble. They must be taught to recognize sin for what it is—a violation of God's holy standards and the source of all of mankind's spiritual, physical, and emotional calamities.

• They need to know that Christ came to deal with both the punishment, practice, and effects of sin. They must become aware of the need for biblical repentance from their sins. And they desperately need to know that through Christ's atoning sacrifice, they can receive forgiveness and cleansing. Someone has remarked that our mental institutions could be almost emptied if their patients could experience forgiveness and have their guilt removed.

• They must be given hope—hope that their lives can be radically changed by the Gospel, that they can learn to function in society and have a reason for living. Many of these people have never known hope or have long ago lost it. We are there to instill that hope into their lives.

• They must get into the Word of God frequently. The Spirit of God works through the revealed will of God. We must teach them to pray as they open their Bibles, asking God to clear away the scales from their eyes so they can behold the wondrous message of the Scriptures.

• They will need the rich fellowship and support of a caring local body. For you to counsel with them, this should, in time, be made a requirement.

• Assign some partners who will help you hold them accountable. Trying to do it all alone may be attempting more than you can effectively accomplish.

• As you counsel with these people, give them regular, meaningful assignments of a practical nature. These may be reading assignments, going to others to restore broken relationships, jotting down where they have sinned in particular ways in order to ask for forgiveness, taking care of tasks that they have neglected or about which they have procrastinated, and compiling lists of things in their lives they want to correct. Well-thought-out assignments can be very beneficial in helping counselees get their lives back on track.

Whether they complete assignments will also help you know if they are serious about genuine change.

• Your actual sessions with them must get to the truth about their lives. Let them know that you cannot and will not spend your time with anyone who lies to you. Otherwise you are spinning your wheels and wasting valuable time that could be used with those who are more serious about their counseling.

• Let them know that you expect progress—not perfection, but progress. This means that you will not allow an open-ended series of sessions that accomplishes nothing. Some people love to just talk to counselors but have no real plans to do what it takes to change their lives. It doesn't take very long to find out who means business.

Your sessions with counselees and the direction you take will depend upon their particular problems. You must be kind but absolutely frank. Your counsel must be firmly rooted in the Word of God, and you should show them where the Bible addresses their situation.

It is wonderful when a church has additional trained counselors who can take the Word of God and help you address the many counseling needs of those who come to you. Some churches have trained counseling teams, and others have separate counseling ministries that use the church facilities.

There will be instances in which we will want to refer counselees to medical personnel or to others who are trained to deal with specific problems. But we should never use referrals as an excuse to keep from calling people to repentance when there are clearly sin issues to be resolved.

We must be prepared to accept the fact that we cannot help every one. Some will continue with their reprehensible behavior and possibly become worse as time passes. But for those who are serious about change, we will receive deep satisfaction in seeing their lives put back together.

In the two verses quoted above, God has called on us to counsel one another and has promised that through the revelation of His truth (in His written Word) we have everything we need for life and godliness. We must know His Word, secure the necessary training, and trust that His Word works—that He can change totally shattered lives. If He can raise people from the dead, He can certainly change the living! What a joy it is to be involved when that occurs.

☙

WHEN TO REFER
THERE MAY BE OTHER HELP OUT THERE

The heart of the discerning acquires knowledge; the ears of the wise seek it out.   —PROVERBS 18:15

The fall of man through Adam's representative sin has resulted in a whole host of problems for us. We are born with a sinful nature. We sin. We experience physical pain and suffering. And we die. Adam got us into a real mess. By our sinful nature and with bodies that are subject to deterioration, we continue in that mode. And because our bodies and our spiritual beings are so interwoven in this life, sometimes physical problems cause or contribute to our spiritual problems. The reverse is also true—spiritual problems sometimes affect us physically.

That reality poses problems for pastors who are trying to help people faced with serious physical or spiritual problems. The Scriptures tell us that God's "power has given us everything we need for life and godliness through our knowledge of him . . ." (2 Peter 1:3). Yet pastors are usually lacking when it comes to medical or physiological issues. Fortunately, others have been better trained to deal with those areas of the human predicament.

When we suspect a physical problem or cannot isolate a spiritual problem that is contributing to or causing a person's malaise, we must not hesitate to see that they contact a physician for analysis and possible help. In the case of certain physical addictions, once we have made it clear that these addictions are sinful and need to be forsaken, we can direct them to other services/counselors for additional assistance.

Often we are afraid of outside services, but some are much better trained in these areas and can come alongside us to assist in helping our counselees in their battle to overcome their addictions. Obviously these services should never be encouraged as a replacement for the Word of God or used as a substitute for the church, but within certain parameters they can be helpful. Many of the people working with these services have suffered the same addictions and have been delivered from them. Their personal experiences and advice can be helpful to our counselees.

Our ministries will often involve both the body and soul of a person simply because they are so interwoven.

In order to use these services safely, the pastor needs to compile a list of them in his own locality, personally visit with them to become aware of their positions and methods, as well as individuals involved, and then determine which ones he could recommend to his counselees. It is also a good thing to encourage key members of his congregation to get involved in some of these ministries. By doing so they may make a connection between the service and the church and thereby help direct the service toward using biblical solutions.

Our ministries will often involve both the body and soul of a person simply because they are so interwoven. Often when people hurt in one of these areas, the other is also affected. Each contributes to the other. Therefore we must be prepared to maximize our ministry to the whole person.

SUICIDE
A PERMANENT SOLUTION TO A TEMPORARY PROBLEM

No man must let the tenant out of the tenement till God the landlord calls for it.   —Thomas Adams

No creature but man willingly kills itself.   —Thomas Watson

The signs were there, but few of us saw them. We all knew he suffered from serious depression, but after all, he had made a profession of faith. He was coming to church regularly. He attended our Bible studies and our home fellowship groups. It is true that he often talked about his loneliness and his lack of joy. Several of us spent a lot of time with him. He was intelligent, polite, generous, well-mannered, and thoughtful of others. Despite the fact that he was raised in an entirely different culture and religious environment, he seemed to be comfortable around us and genuinely appeared to desire our company.

That's what was so odd. After he met with a fellowship group in our home one Wednesday evening he went home and ended his life violently with a firearm.

We later learned that he had talked about suicide with his family on many occasions since his beloved wife had died from cancer and his son had become paralyzed from a motorcycle accident. Though we all knew he was depressed at times, none of us ever thought he might destroy himself. How we wished that his family had told us just how seriously depressed he was.

Nevertheless, in retrospect the telltale signs were there for us. Though many suicides appear to be spur-of-the-moment actions, most follow a long period of depression and even discussion about suicide.

For many years I grew up with the sentiment that "if someone talks about suicide, you can be sure the person won't go through with it." That's a false and dangerous position. My experience with depressed people is that when they have suffered from long periods of depression and begin to talk about suicide, we had better pay attention. Having been associated with several individuals through the years who have attempted suicide, I now know that such talk can be serious.

We should not have been caught by surprise as we all were when our friend was found dead the next morning. We must take our members' talk and mood swings seriously, and we must be prepared to offer them the help they need or to direct them to those more capable of addressing their problems.

MAKING JUDGMENTS
GATHER ALL THE FACTS

When justice is done, it brings joy to the righteous but terror to evildoers. —PROVERBS 21:15

We are going to be called on to render our judgment on a whole range of issues in our congregation. Is a certain person qualified to teach? Is a particular plan or program better than an alternative? Is a member really a believer? Is a certain matter private, or should it be discussed publicly? Is this the right time to institute a building plan or should it be later? Has this person repented? Is it time for the church to exercise the discipline of a particular member?

Both the church leaders and the laymen will want to know our judgments in all sorts of issues. There will be times when we would prefer not to make a judgment, but we cannot escape the necessity of taking a position.

Because our position will influence and affect so many people, we must use the best possible judgment. Many times it will not be a simple matter of right and wrong, but which is the better choice of several possible and legitimate options.

How, then, do we render judgment? Here are some common-sense steps:

- We must pray about the matter, asking God to work in our minds so that we do not overlook any important, relevant matter.
- We must gather all the available facts. That requires patience and work. To not do so is to invite disaster and to lose our influence with the congregation and our fellow leaders.
- We must settle the question of whether or not the Scriptures give us clear guidance. If so, no further judgment is necessary. We must simply follow the Word of God.
- When the situation allows, we need to test our judgment before it is made public. That can be done by discussing it at length with our fellow leaders or with confidants, inviting them to critically assess our position.

As leaders we will be called on to lead and to set the tone for the congregation. As we make wise decisions, our congregations will learn to follow our leadership and support our ministries.

There will be times when we discover that our judgment was wrong. As soon as that has been firmly established, we need to admit it and correct any action based on the wrong judgment. Congregations will readily follow leaders who are honest and open to correction.

FOR ADDITIONAL STUDY

The Word of God and Counseling

Psalms 1:1-3; 119
Proverbs 1:25, 30-33
Proverbs 8:14
Proverbs 12:15
Proverbs 13:10
Proverbs 15:22
Proverbs 19:20-21
Proverbs 20:18
Proverbs 27:9
Matthew 18:15-18
Luke 6:46-49

Luke 11:28
John 5:39
Rom. 15:14
1 Corinthians 3:19
2 Corinthians 11:28-29
Galatians 6:1-2
Ephesians 5:18-19
Colossians 2:2-3; 3:16
1 Thessalonians 4:18
1 Thessalonians 5:11

1 Timothy 5:1-2
2 Timothy 3:15-17
Titus 2:1-15
Hebrews 3:12-14
Hebrews 4:12-13
Hebrews 10:25
Hebrews 12:14-17
James 1:19-25
James 5:16
2 Peter 1:3-4

WEDDINGS, DIVORCES, FUNERALS

Marriages
SOMETIMES WE MUST SAY NO

Do not be yoked together with unbelievers. For what do righteousness and wickedness have in common? Or what fellowship can light have with darkness? —2 CORINTHIANS 6:14

Marriage ceremonies can be wonderful events. To see two godly people join together into the basic building block of society can be a thrilling event for a pastor. Two deliriously happy people, committed to the Lord's service, with godly families and friends around them, create a happy occasion for everyone.

There are times, however, when a proposed marriage can be an absolute nightmare for the pastor. Unequally yoked couples will come to us for marriage—one being a believer and the other an unbeliever. Others will come to us from previous marriages with no biblical grounds for their divorce. Some will be too young and immature to understand the commitment involved in marriage. Others will come promising to become involved in your church if you will perform their ceremony; but once it is completed, you never see them again. Deeply

---

We must be prepared to sometimes say no firmly but gently and to explain the biblical standards for marriage.

---

committed adult members of your congregation will ask you to perform the ceremony for their son or daughter who is madly in love with a lost person, or a person from another church with a questionable understanding of the Scriptures. Others will call on you to marry them without your having time to counsel them. You will be asked to perform the ceremony for people who have absolutely no relationship to

Christ or to any church. And sad to say, in our culture you may even be requested to perform homosexual or lesbian marriages.

We must be prepared to sometimes say no firmly but gently and to explain the biblical standards for marriage. While there may be a difference of opinion as to whether the Scriptures allow divorce and remarriage under any circumstances, the pastor must have established his standards before the requests for his services come, and he must let the church know those standards during his candidacy so they are fully aware of his position.

In most churches these situations will be routine, but you and your church leadership need to be in agreement on a firm biblical position on these very important issues.

SEPARATIONS
ARE THERE BIBLICAL GROUNDS?

Marriage should be honored by all, and the marriage bed kept pure.
—HEBREWS 13:4

What advice should a pastor give when a husband and a wife are professing believers and the husband is physically beating the wife and children? Can the wife separate from her husband? What about when the wife is a compulsive spender or gambler and keeps plunging the family deeper and deeper into debt? Can the husband separate and cut her off from the family funds? What advice does a pastor give a couple who has received counsel for years and yet they fight daily, keeping the children in turmoil? Is a temporary separation permissible?

What about when a wife learns that her husband has been unfaithful to her for years with numerous partners and she is now worried that she might contract an infectious disease, even AIDS, from her husband? She wants a separation until she knows he is clear of such diseases. Further, she thinks she needs time to determine if he is now repentant, and she comes to us for counsel. Are we on legitimate biblical grounds to say she can have some time away from him to help determine these important areas?

What about a situation where the husband stays out most nights without a good explanation as to where he has been, comes home drunk, will not work, and does not provide any help to his wife who has to work outside the home to pay their bills? She is the one who has to raise the children and keep up the home. May she separate from her husband until he genuinely changes? What about the man who irresponsibly refuses to hold down a job, putting the family into terrible debt, ruining both his and his wife's credit reputation, and seeming to have no desire to correct this pattern? Must the wife continue to subject herself to these situations?

The Scriptures teach us that there is much wisdom in the advice of multiple counselors.

These, and other examples like them, are common problems in the world today, even among professed believers. And the elder/pastor will find the buck stopping at his desk when it comes to determining what the Bible says in these areas. The Bible gives us excellent principles, but in specific cases we sometimes do not have explicit answers to address every detail of the situation. What we do have, however, are godly men who are in positions of leadership within the congregation who can wrestle through the specifics of each case and help us come to a conclusion. The Scriptures teach us that there is much wisdom in the advice of multiple counselors.

In general, separations should occur only as a last resort. But there are times when one's life, children, or sanity are involved, and the seemingly prudent thing to do is to allow for a temporary separation with the hope expressed that the guilty party will repent of his/her actions and the marriage will be saved.

DIVORCES
WE MUST HAVE A BIBLICAL POSITION

"I hate divorce," says the LORD *God of Israel.* —MALACHI 2:16

Unfortunately, divorces occur even among Christians. And divorced people will come to us wanting to get married. With over half of the marriages in our country ending up in divorce, this becomes an issue about which we must have a biblical position.

Is a Christian ever allowed to seek a divorce? May a Christian remarry following a divorce? If so, under what circumstances? What is permissible for a Christian who has been deserted by his or her spouse? What is Jesus really saying about marriage and divorce in Matthew 5 and Matthew 19? These and other complicated questions arise often for a pastor. He therefore needs to have a clear understanding of what the Lord allows and commands.

First, we know from the verse quoted above that God hates divorce. He hates it because it violates His perfect blending of a husband and wife to create the basic cornerstone of society, a family. When a family breaks up, all sorts of evil breaks out. God also hates divorce because he foresees the many hurts that the entire family will face. And He hates divorce because often that example extends to the children, and in some cases the children's children. It seems to create an endless cycle of hurt, anger, and recrimination.

Second, God never encourages divorce. He simply allows it under certain circumstances where the marriage bond has been so broken that the pieces cannot be put back together, particularly by sexual unfaithfulness.

Third, God allows divorce when one spouse deserts the other because he or she does not want to live with a Christian (1 Corinthians 7:15).

To be more specific, here is what I think God is telling us

regarding divorce and remarriage: In the case of persistent, unrepentant *porneia* (illicit sexual behavior with a man, woman, or beast), the innocent party may seek a divorce. He or she is not required to divorce but may do so if there is persistent behavior of this type. Or if an unbeliever is married to a believer, and the unbeliever does not wish to continue to live with the believer and deserts the spouse, then the believer may complete the legal requirements to formally end the marriage. In that case, it is the nonbeliever who has deserted the spouse; therefore, the nonbeliever is the one who has, in effect, brought about the divorce. The innocent party, having been deserted, is simply carrying out the legal implications of the divorce.

In all of these cases, if genuine repentance occurs in the life of the guilty party, the innocent party should be quick to forgive and refrain from dissolving the marriage. In the case of *porneia*, should there be persistent occurrences, the innocent party must before God seek to determine the legitimacy of the repentance. If it is judged that the repentance is only lip service and not heartfelt, the innocent party has the right under Jesus' words to go through with the divorce.

In the case of either persistent *porneia* or desertion, the innocent party not only has the right to dissolve the marriage but is also free to remarry.

I realize that some disagree with this position. It is not easy to know the exact mind of the Lord in these areas, especially when marital differences become extremely complicated. However, the pastoral staff, along with the entire church leadership, must work in unison from a basic framework so that when a divorce occurs everyone will understand the church's position.

With the divorce rate in our culture so unfortunately high, even among Christians, we will face these issues regularly. Therefore we must have clear positions on the subjects of marriage, divorce, and remarriage.

THE WEDDING SERVICE
TIME-CONSUMING BUT FULL OF OPPORTUNITIES

Anyone can build a house; we need the Lord for the creation of a home.   —JOHN HENRY JOWETT

One year I was called on to perform a wedding service on December 20, then another one on December 25 (Christmas day!), and then another one on December 27. With all the rehearsals, actual ceremonies, and receptions, by the end of the last one I was worn out with weddings!

With the weeks of premarital counseling that have to take place, the planning of the service itself, the preparation for the service, the rehearsal dinner, the service, the picture-taking sessions, and finally the reception, a wedding can be a time- and energy-absorbing event for a pastor. But it can also be time well spent if properly used.

I can think of three particular times during the wedding process that are great opportunities to get God's message across. The first is during the premarital counseling sessions. There is so little understanding today about marital responsibilities by young people. Basic information about *agape* love, leadership, submissiveness, forgiveness, forbearance, good communication, sacrifice, spiritual unity, lifetime commitments, Christian family values, sexual fidelity, stewardship, financial responsibility, and child-rearing must be covered during those times with the love-struck couple. You just hope they catch some of what you are trying to tell them. They are probably not going to hear these things in any other context before they become husband and wife. These sessions can be wonderful opportunities to teach them practical issues in these and other areas before the knot is tied. Of particular importance to be stressed, over and over again, is that they are entering into a lifetime commitment!

The second opportunity for the pastor to convey God's message is when the families are together for the rehearsal session and the dinner that follows. At those times the role and importance of family life can be emphasized. Often there will be members of the family present who are unconverted. The way we conduct ourselves, greet the family members, and explain the importance and blessings of a Christian marriage can help attract those lost people to Christ.

Third, attending the wedding service will be people from different professions, backgrounds, and religious affiliations. Our wedding messages can weave the Gospel in by demonstrating how Christ loved the church and gave Himself for her. In the same way He calls on husbands to love their brides and be willing to make sacrifices for them. There may be some people in the audience for the first and last time hearing the Gospel.

They are entering into a lifetime commitment!

Weddings take a lot of our time. Those three weddings I conducted in eight days kept me busy. Then on top of that, our oldest son surprised us by marrying his sweetheart that same year on December 29 (two days after the last of my three weddings).

It was a good thing that I was not involved in that wedding (it took place in a courthouse in a distant state) because I might have been tempted to convince them to delay the event until I caught my breath. They called to tell us they were married, concerned that we might feel hurt because we were not asked to participate and because the wedding took place in a public facility rather than in a church building. They were surprised to learn that I was in full agreement with their action (and I didn't mind not having to officiate at a fourth wedding in ten days!).

Weddings can put us into contact with a number of people whom we would probably never meet otherwise. For that reason alone, the time and energy spent can be very rewarding and useful.

FUNERALS
SAD BUT WONDERFUL OPPORTUNITIES

"Where, O death, is your victory? Where, O death, is your sting?"
The sting of death is sin, and the power of sin is the law. But thanks
be to God! He gives us the victory through our Lord Jesus Christ.
—1 CORINTHIANS 15:55-57

If sinners will be damned, at least let them leap to hell over our bodies.
—CHARLES H. SPURGEON

Probably the saddest funeral I have conducted was when those who attended were not sad at all. A woman in her sixties, who had no immediate family members, was being buried by her extended family. They had her body cremated, wanted the cheapest funeral service possible, and wanted me to keep my remarks as brief as possible. Apart from me, there were seven people in attendance. The family wanted to dispose of her body the easiest, quickest way. Their attendance at the funeral seemed totally perfunctory. I could see neither grief nor remorse in anyone. I was called because a member of the family who lived in our neighborhood suggested my name. What saddened me most was that this woman lived over sixty years in this life and apparently influenced very few people, if any. No one seemed upset by her death.

Not knowing either the deceased or most of the other members of the family, I felt it was appropriate to simply talk about death, judgment, and eternity and then to explain the Gospel. Several of the family members seemed a bit stunned, but I looked on it as a sad but wonderful opportunity to talk to the living rather than the dead. I tried to be kind and gentle, but straightforward and earnest. And I prayed hard that God would convict someone in that small group to reassess his/her life in view of eternity.

Other funerals have been occasions for rejoicing rather than times of sadness. When our loved ones and friends die who are believers, tremendous opportunities arise to talk about death having no sting for the Christian. We can remind the listeners that it is superior for the believer when he departs this life to go be with Christ. We will miss them in this life, but we know that the day will come when we will rejoice together with them in heaven. Such funerals are times for celebration.

Most people do not want to think about death and eternity. Yet, unless the Lord comes in the meantime, everyone who is born is going to die. There is an absolute one to one ratio! We cannot escape that logic. So the death of a family member, friend, or someone close to us is a sudden, jarring wake-up call. And when people are thinking about the finality of death, there is a wonderful opportunity to preach the Gospel.

As people are dying, family members and friends gather around them, either in their homes or hospital rooms. Then when the death occurs, family and friends gather in a home to help the bereaved family. Sometimes there is a formal visitation period at the funeral home, usually the night before the funeral. On the day of the funeral there will be two more events—the funeral itself and then the final interment at the cemetery. At all of these events the people who gather are thinking about death. Those times are available to us to gently but boldly talk to people about their lives and their need to trust in Christ.

I can well remember a friend of mine sitting in a living room where the family had gathered following the suicide of a mother. My friend began talking to an uncle about the Gospel, and the conversation became somewhat combative. He made no headway with the uncle, but unknown to him, a son-in-law of the deceased woman was quietly listening to the conversation. As that man judged his own life, he realized he was in danger of eternal destruction. The Lord began to work quietly in his heart. The Spirit opened his heart, and he was saved; his wife and children were later saved too. Many of his extended family members came to embrace the Gospel, and his witness has caused many others to evaluate their status before Almighty God.

It all started with a sad, unexpected suicide. Yet God used that time to start the growth of the Gospel in that family. Tremendous fruit developed from that one occasion.

When someone dies, much immediate support and comfort is usually given to the loved ones left behind. Usually that show of concern continues up to and perhaps right after the funeral. But within a day or so after the funeral people begin to stop calling and dropping by to show their love and concern. That is when the finality of death sets in and when the loneliness and grief is most felt. Here is where we can help. We can encourage others to keep in contact with those who are left behind (and can do so ourselves). It has been said that the worst times for the spouse or family (particularly if they now live alone) are the weeks after the funeral. We should make visits during these times and encourage our members to also regularly keep in contact with the grieving family. These may be wonderful times to talk about life and death and the hope we have of the resurrection and reunion with God's people.

Funerals occur regularly. Sometimes they are times of rejoicing. Sometimes they are very sad. But they are always wonderful opportunities!

꿈

FOR ADDITIONAL STUDY

Marriage/Divorce

Genesis 2:18-25	Matthew 19:3-12	1 Corinthians 7:1-40
Deuteronomy 22:13-30	Mark 10:2-12	Ephesians 5:22-33
Deuteronomy 24:1-5	Luke 20:27-36	1 Timothy 5:1-16
Proverbs 2:16-22	John 3:29	Hebrews 13:4
Malachi 2:14-16	Romans 7:1-3	1 Peter 3:1-7
Matthew 5:31-32		

Death/Judgment

Genesis 2:17	John 8:51	2 Thessalonians 1:6-9
Genesis 3:19	John 11:1-44	2 Timothy 1:10
Job 3:16-19	Acts 5:5, 10	Hebrews 2:15
Psalms 9:17	Acts 24:15	Hebrews 9:27
Psalms 104:29	Romans 1:18, 32	Hebrews 11:35-37
Proverbs 14:12	Romans 2:8-9	James 1:15; 4:12
Ecclesiastes 8:8	Romans 5:12-21	James 5:20
Ecclesiastes 9:5-10	Romans 9:22	2 Peter 1:13-15
Matthew 10:28	1 Corinthians 15:20-21, 26	2 Peter 2:12, 17
Matthew 23:33-35	1 Corinthians 15:35-37	Revelation 1:18
Luke 12:20-21	2 Corinthians 5:1	Revelation 2:11
Luke 20:35-36	Philippians 1:21-23	Revelation 20:5-6
Luke 23:19-31	1 Thessalonians 1:10	Revelation 21:4
John 3:18		

Resurrection

Job 19:26	Psalms 16:10	Psalms 49:15
Isaiah 26:19	Daniel 12:13	Hosea 13:14
Matthew 9:25	Matthew 22:29-32	Matthew 27:53
Mark 12:24-27	Luke 7:14-15	Luke 14:14
John 5:28-29	John 6:35-40	John 11:1-44
John 12:24	Acts 4:2	Acts 17:18
Acts 24:15	Acts 26:8	1 Corinthians 15:1-58
2 Corinthians 5:1	Philippians 3:11, 21	Colossians 3:4
1 Thessalonians 4:13—5:11	Hebrews 6:2	Hebrews 11:35
1 John 3:2-3	Revelation 20:6, 13.	

Section Eight

RELATIONSHIPS

WITH OTHERS

Mentoring
PASSING ALONG THE TORCH

He [Paul] came to Derbe and then to Lystra, where a disciple named Timothy lived. . . . Paul wanted to take him along on the journey, so he circumcised him. —ACTS 16:1-3

I have no one else like him [Timothy], who takes a genuine interest in your welfare. For everyone looks out for his own interests, not those of Jesus Christ. But you know that Timothy has proved himself, because as a son with his father he has served with me in the work of the gospel. —PHILIPPIANS 2:20-22

Some ten or more years passed between Acts 16 and Philippians 2. Between those two dates a very significant mentoring took place by Paul of this young disciple, Timothy. Paul knew he was passing off the scene, and he was preparing to place the mantle of Christianity upon his young disciple. In fact, in Paul's last letter, 2 Timothy, he indeed does pass the torch to Timothy, giving him, as it were, last-minute instructions about preaching the whole counsel of God and standing firm against the enemies of Christ.

In the case involving Timothy, the mentoring was apparently very well done. It had actually begun with his grandmother and mother, Lois and Eunice (2 Timothy 1:5) and was continued by Paul. Apparently after Paul had passed off the scene, Timothy was released from prison (Hebrews 13:23), indicating that he had, in fact, remained firm and had been imprisoned for the sake of the Gospel.

We are all called to mentor someone. A mother may mentor her children or younger women, or a father trains his son or a neighbor. A mature layman can mentor a new believer. A youth pastor could choose a few of his youth to personally disciple. A pastor could look for men with potential into whom he could literally pour his life. A seminary professor could, in addition to his class lectures, choose a few young men to personally mentor during their years at the school.

This mentoring should involve grounding another person in the basics of the Gospel, in theological concepts, in how to live as a husband, father, faithful employee, evangelist, or in other relationships. We could demonstrate to others how to teach the Bible. Sometimes it can be simply a matter of telling others what we know about the truths of Scripture. Anyone can do that. In fact, John MacArthur once gave some advice that has stuck with me for years. It went something like this: "There is bound to be some person on this earth who knows less than you do about Christ. Find that person and tell him what you know." That is so simple that anyone can do it.

The best example of mentoring took place in those three years in which Christ taught His disciples. Paul must have followed that example during the ten or more years he spent with Timothy.

There is one concern that needs to be expressed about the mentoring process—a caution both to the mentor and the person being taught. Occasionally a student blindly follows his mentor and thereby is led into heretical positions or wrong behavior. This is how cults begin. A mentor with a strong or magnetic personality will develop a following, and before long a full-blown schism or sect has begun. Often the followers will, in time, move further away from the truth and even become worse than the leader.

That places a responsibility on both parties. Every step along the way must be squarely based upon the Scriptures. As teachers (and mentors) we will be judged more strictly—with the Word of God as the standard.

We never grow too old to be mentored or to be a mentor. We can look upon ourselves as middlemen. We should place ourselves under someone wiser and more knowledgeable than ourselves in order to learn from them, then be looking for those to whom we can transmit what we have learned. The torch must be passed continuously from one generation to the next.

〜

AN INDEPENDENT SPIRIT
WE NEED OTHERS

There is no doubt but that if there be one God, there is but one church; if there is but one Christ, there is but one church; if there be but one cross, there is but one church; if there be but one Holy Ghost, there is but one church.   —A. A. HODGE

I began my ministry in a denominational church but later became pastor of an independent body and retired as executive pastor of a well-respected, independent congregation. Both denominational and independent churches have their strengths and their weaknesses. Without going into the reasons, I prefer an independent body. But I have absolutely no problems with my brothers in Christ who prefer to serve in evangelical, denominational congregations.

There is a difference between a person who serves in an independent congregation and one who has an "independent spirit." By the latter I mean those pastors who will not fellowship with other pastors and churches, who cut themselves off from all activities with other believers, and who refuse to learn anything from those who are not a part of their own congregation. They seem to be afraid they will be tainted by something bad in the lives and activities of other believers.

This isolation will surely retard the growth of the Gospel in that particular geographical area. It obscures the unity of the body of Christ. It tells the world that Christians are not one in spirit. Not having fellowship with and learning from other brothers and sisters in Christ stunts the spiritual growth of that pastor and congregation.

Conservative, evangelical churches have many basics in common—a commitment to the inspired, inerrant Word of God, the divinity of Christ, salvation by grace through faith alone, the reality of heaven and hell, the necessity of spiritual growth and godliness, to mention just a few. There is much rich fellowship to be enjoyed when fellow believers are committed to these principles, even though we may be in different congregations or denominations.

Local churches can also accomplish much more when they join forces to promote God-honoring activities. Among these are local ministries to the poor, area evangelistic teams, joint Bible conferences, Reformation weekends, pulpit vacation supply, social programs designed to help neighborhoods, ministries designed to provide alternatives to abortion, joint support of Christians who run for public office, multi-church picnics and other outings, and joint prayer meetings. There are so many things we can do to be a solid, collective witness to our community.

Local churches can also accomplish much more when they join forces to promote God-honoring activities.

In each geographical area there should be evangelical ministerial associations in which the pastors can get to know each other. From those gatherings can spring the plans to help churches work together and thereby unify the universal body of Christ. The more fractured we are, the greater we become spectacles to the world. The more we are united in love, the more the world sees of Christ.

This unity, of course, must not be a unity in darkness, but rather a unity based on the cardinal doctrines of our faith. A good example of that would be the comparatively new Alliance of Confessing Evangelicals, which brings together evangelicals of many different backgrounds, including both denominational and nondenominational pastors and churches.

EVANGELISM/OUTREACH
IF WE DON'T EVANGELIZE,
THE FLOCK MAY FOLLOW OUR EXAMPLE

Evangelism is the perpetual task of the whole church, and not the peculiar hobby of certain of its members.   —E. WILSON CARLISLE

We are to evangelize, not because it is easy, not because we may be successful, but because Christ has called us. He is our Lord. We have no other choice, but to obey him.   —LEIGHTON FORD

But you, keep your head in all situations, endure hardship, do the work of an evangelist, discharge all the duties of your ministry.
    —2 TIMOTHY 4:5

It is hypocritical to teach and preach to our congregation about its duty to evangelize if we, its pastors, do not do so. Since most of our time as pastors is spent with believers, we must arrange our schedules to put ourselves in contact with lost people on a regular basis.

Actually, we are in contact with unbelievers regularly through our normal, everyday activities. The service station attendant, the checkout clerk at the grocery store, the woman who works for the cleaners, the serviceperson who works on our automobiles or air conditioning system, just to mention a few. These are wonderful day-to-day opportunities to speak a word about the Gospel, to leave a tract, to pass along a Scripture portion or New Testament.

Another way to spread the Gospel is to enclose a tract every time we pay a bill, or to leave tracts at the Post Office counter as we collect our mail or purchase stamps. These tracts should be attractive, simple, and informative with a clear presentation. Always put your name, address, and phone number on the tract so people can follow up for additional spiritual guidance. These activities are simple and easy everyday ways we can spread the Gospel.

Other more formal approaches by which we make specific plans to meet people and to follow up on a long-term basis require more planning and effort. We can plan activities or join groups to meet and get to know lost people around us. We can join a tennis league, a golf course, a discussion group, a hunting camp, a jogging team, an exercise program, a softball or racquetball league, a touring schedule, a service project for the poor, a volunteer fire department, or many other entities or informal groups.

As we become acquainted with people, trusting relationships begin to develop. We can invite them to our home for a meal, plan trips with them, and shop with them. In these ways we begin to open the door of communication so we can talk to them about the Gospel.

Another very effective way to reach the lost is to take the lead in a community Bible class in our neighborhood. Subjects such as an "Introduction to the Bible," "Is the Bible Reliable?" "Religions of the World," or studies of New Testament books (such as the Gospel of John or the book of Romans) can be extremely effective in creating interest and eventually confronting people with the Gospel. In my own experience with home classes in the book of Romans I have been blessed by seeing a number of people embrace Christ as they for the first time understood justification by faith.

The point is to look for every possible opportunity to meet and influence the lost. We have the only message that can bring spiritual light and life into the world of darkness.

As our congregation sees us witnessing in this manner, and as they see conversions taking place, it is only natural for them to follow our example. We need to involve them in this endeavor, show them the way, then watch their progress. The results can be something wonderful to behold.

If we, their pastors, do not set the example for them, we should not expect, and certainly cannot command, that they evangelize the lost. To be obedient in this area will take planning and much work, but the angels will be rejoicing in heaven when sinners repent.

ᕫᕫ

OUR PUBLIC INVOLVEMENT
THE COMMUNITY NEEDS TO KNOW WE ARE AROUND

"You are the salt of the earth. But if the salt loses its saltiness, how can it be made salty again? It is no longer good for anything, except to be thrown out and trampled by men. You are the light of the world. A city on a hill cannot be hidden. Neither do people light a lamp and put it under a bowl. Instead they put it on its stand, and it gives light to everyone in the house. In the same way, let your light shine before men, that they may see your good deeds and praise your Father in heaven."   —MATTHEW 5:13-16

Sometimes a church and her pastor are so concerned with their own members, congregational needs, and problems that they tend to forget they are called to minister to those around them. In fact, Jesus calls us to be salt and light in a dark, confused world. When Jesus said that, He was using terms that were pregnant with meaning. By using these examples He calls on us to be busy influencing the lost world around us. Salt preserves, flavors, irritates, permeates, makes thirsty, heals, and attracts. Light dispels darkness, illuminates, cheers, warms, guides, removes fear, reflects, and attracts.

The world we live in is a dark, guilty, sick, lost, and joyless society. Most people do not know why they are here on this planet or what life is all about. Most of them are born, live, and die with absolutely no rhyme or reason for their existence. And as they live their lives, their spiritual deadness comes out in many forms. We therefore are to speak up with the truth that alone can dispel darkness and illuminate their lives. In fact, Paul says we are to shine as brilliant stars in a dark universe (Phil. 2:15-16).

There is no way we can do this while remaining isolated from others. We must form friendships and associations with the lost, invite them into our homes, attend various events with them, speak at some of their functions, and minister to some of their physical needs.

We can also join forces with other evangelical Christians to inaugurate ministries that help meet the needs of the poor—home building programs; soup kitchens; clean-up, paint-up, fix-up campaigns; ministries such as crisis pregnancy centers; and many others.

Along with our other brothers and sisters in Christ, we can speak up and be heard on a whole range of moral and social issues. Evangelical ministerial associations can and should be recognized in each location so we can be heard regularly on a whole range of issues with which society deals.

Pastors can also join organizations such as a Lions Club, Kiwanis, or an Optimist Club where they can meet and influence people in their community whom they might otherwise never meet.

Using these many opportunities to be around the lost will give us an entrée into their lives that will provide natural occasions to present the Gospel to them. The Gospel is the ultimate salt and light. It alone will dispel the darkness and preserve men's souls for all eternity.

JEALOUSY AND COMPETITION
WE ARE ON THE SAME TEAM!

It is true that some preach Christ out of envy and rivalry, but others out of good will. The latter do so in love, knowing that I am put here for the defense of the gospel. The former preach Christ out of selfish ambition, not sincerely, supposing that they can stir up trouble for me while I am in chains. But what does it matter? The important thing is that in every way, whether from false motives or true, Christ is preached. And because of this I rejoice. —PHILIPPIANS 1:15-18

Let's face it. We struggle with sins daily—*our* sins! And two of those sins are jealousy of and competition with other ministries. By "other ministries" I would include other pastors, churches, mission works, and parachurch ministries. These sins can manifest themselves in any number of situations. A ministry grows more rapidly than ours, has a new or better program than we have, or gets our uninvolved members to serve with them. Perhaps members leave our ministry and join them; or our church is struggling financially while others seem to have enough money even to expand. It can happen. It does happen.

We sometimes make innuendoes about some of their theological views, we question their sincerity, we point out weaknesses, we question their methods, and we slander them. We attempt to build ourselves up by tearing them down.

The tragic thing is that we are often targeting people who are our brothers, people who are on Christ's team. Many of these people are genuinely a part of Christ's body, those for whom He effectually bled and died.

Paul faced that problem when he was under house arrest in Rome. Evangelical pastors in Rome were jealous of Paul's successes, but Paul did not strike back. Instead, he expressed thankfulness that the Gospel was being preached and people were responding.

Perhaps therein lies the key as to how we should respond. Are these other ministries evangelical? Are they preaching the Gospel? If so, we must be extremely careful that we neither say nor do anything that would take away from their successes.

In the end we will reign in heaven with them. We will bow together before the throne. We have read the end of the book, and we know that we will win, together. They are our brothers, not our enemies. Our Lord said, "If they are not against us, they are for us."

Before we say anything against a brother or his ministry, we must examine our hearts very carefully. Are we striking out from our own jealousy or competitive spirit? Or are we genuinely concerned about our own flock and any influence that would harm their souls?

Jealousy can also be an issue between staff members in the same local body. To see others around us succeed in their ministries should, instead, cause us to rejoice because it benefits the church. When our focus is on the growth of the body and the glory of Christ, we will have no room for jealousy and competition.

STANDING ALONE

SOMETIMES WE MAY BE VERY ALONE!

Unless I am convinced by the testimonies of the Holy Scripture or evident reason (for I believe neither in the Pope nor councils alone, since it has been established that they have often erred and contradicted themselves), I am bound by the Scriptures adduced by me, and my conscience has been taken captive by the Word of God, and I am neither able nor willing to recant, since it is neither safe nor right to act against conscience. God help me. Amen. —MARTIN LUTHER

These words spoken by Martin Luther in 1521 before the Diet of Worms unleashed the Protestant Reformation, during which salvation by grace through faith alone was firmly established as the truth of the Word of God. With only a few people around him, Luther stood essentially alone against the false theology and the ungodly practices of the Roman Catholic Church. Had Luther recanted and denied the truth, the church today might still be trying to recapture the true Gospel.

In our day also, pastors must at times stand boldly on crucial issues, and doing so may isolate us. It is not popular to speak out strongly on issues such as abortion, homosexuality, church discipline, mixed marriages of believers with unbelievers, false teachers, false miracles, or the total inspiration and reliability of the Word of God. When we do, it can be very lonely. Refusing to join hands with those who confuse the Gospel of grace with a gospel of works can make us appear to be bigoted.

But such issues are significant enough (though some other issues are not) that we must drive theological stakes in the ground and say that we cannot move away from them. It hurts to be cut off from others. It hurts to be considered a fanatic or religious bigot. Such phrases will be thrown at us venomously. At times we may even lose our pastorates.

But we must constantly remember whom we are to please. Christ is our Master. The church is His. He gave His truth to His body. He died for her. We cannot for a moment change His Word, alter His plans for His church, or allow practices in His church that He squarely condemns.

We may find ourselves alone with respect to others, but if we are faithful to Christ we are never alone. His approval, His smile, His blessing must be our goal.

Martin Luther's single-minded purpose was to stand on God's truth. He could do no other. Neither can we.

MISSIONS
WE NEED FIRSTHAND KNOWLEDGE
OF THE WORLD OF MISSIONS

Too many Christians are stuffing themselves with gospel blessings while millions have never had a taste.   —VANCE HAVNER

Many of us cannot reach the mission fields on our feet, but we can reach them on our knees.   —T. J. BACH

Every Christian who is not called to preach is called to send other Christians to do so.   —JOHN BLANCHARD

No man is truly awake today who has not developed a supra-national horizon to his thinking. No church is anything more than a pathetic pietistic backwater unless it is first and fundamentally and all the time a world missionary church.   —JAMES S. STEWART

God has blessed American Christians with the opportunity to be able to lead the world in the financial support of missions around the globe. But today more and more missionaries are leaving the fields and are not being replaced. And in many countries missionaries are finding that their visas are not being renewed by the overseas governments, and they are no longer being allowed to return to conduct their ministries openly. And so mission work and the lives of missionaries are changing rapidly worldwide. As pastors, we need to know what is happening so our messages and church programs reflect actual situations.

One of the best ways to keep abreast of current needs and trends on the foreign mission field is to take short-term mission trips with our members and missionaries. My own experiences with trips to Mexico, China, and twice to New Guinea have been absolutely invaluable in my assessment of missionary work. Those trips of two to three weeks each provided me with a glimpse of the actual work in those fields. I could never have understood what I now know just by listening to our missionaries and viewing their slides and videos.

One of the best ways to keep abreast of current needs and trends on the foreign mission field is to take short-term mission trips with our members and missionaries.

Though my knowledge is still very imperfect (you can only learn so much during several trips of a few weeks each), I now know so much better the condition of those being evangelized, the trials and hardships of the people on the field, the ways to both encourage and discourage the missionaries, some of their financial and spiritual needs, the obstacles that present themselves to the mission families, some of the dangers involved, and some of the loneliness encountered by being away from family and friends for extended periods of time. I saw what a letter or package from home meant to them. I have a better appreciation of why they need regular and extended furloughs, why it is vitally important that they keep regular contact with their supporters, and how it hurts them when their support drops while they are away in a distant area.

The need for communication was obvious. I now understand better what it is like to be away from American news broadcasts, newspapers, and other forms of updates about what is going on back home and in the outside world.

Then, too, as our members think they are being called into foreign missions and discuss these matters with us, we will know more fully what they are about to undertake and should be in an improved position to help them assess their qualifications and personal temperaments for that form of ministry.

We should lead the church to choose people to serve on an active missions committee who will help us keep world missions before the congregation. They can plan and manage the missions program of the body. They can keep up with the missionaries and their needs. But as pastors we must realize that the most effective way to promote missions is from the pulpit. If the church leadership is not solidly behind the missions ministry of the church, it will languish in a committee, and the congregation will not be kept aware of the responsibilities and opportunities for worldwide missions.

God has a heart for missions. As pastors in His local bodies, we need that same heart. Visiting the fields will help do that for us.

FOR ADDITIONAL STUDY

Evangelism and Missions

Matthew 28:16-20	Romans 1:16-17	Philippians 2:14-18
Acts 1:7-8	Romans 10:1-21	Colossians 4:2-6
Acts 8:26-40	Romans 11:1-32	2 Thessalonians 3:1
Acts 10:1-48	Ephesians 6:19-20	2 Timothy 4:1-8
Acts 13—28	Philippians 1:12-26	

Section Nine

DANGERS

PROOF-TEXTING
IS THAT REALLY WHAT THE TEXT SAYS?

Watch your . . . doctrine closely. —1 TIMOTHY 4:16

God's Word says "a person is justified by what he does and not by faith alone." Yes, that's what James 2:24 clearly states. You can actually read those words in your New Testament. Is that a misprint? No! Is it a corrupted text? No! Is it a poor translation? No! It's what the text actually says.

The problem with quoting only those biblical words is that there is more said in the immediate context. James is arguing that a man who has a dead faith, a faith that produces no works, has simply a head knowledge and not saving faith. Our faith has to be demonstrated by our works. James uses Abraham as an example of a man with faith who was willing to demonstrate his faith by offering up his son Isaac on the altar. And then James concludes with these statements: "'Abraham believed God, and it was credited to him as righteousness,' and he was called God's friend. You see that a person is justified by what he does and not by faith alone. . . . As the body without the spirit is dead, so faith without deeds is dead" (James 2:23-26).

This example is used simply to spotlight a mistake that is made too often, even by preachers. We, too, have a tendency to lift verses out of their context and use them as proof-texts for what we believe or how we behave. We do this before our congregations and thereby use the Scriptures in a way in which God never intended. God has promised that His Word would accomplish His purpose. But when His words are wrenched from their context and our thoughts are substituted for His thoughts, we should not think God will bless His truth through us. In fact, as teachers we "will be judged more strictly" (James 3:1).

What does that mean for us? It requires that we tie ourselves to our desks until we know what each verse or phrase means. And we should not be forming our theological convictions until we know what God is actually saying in those verses. Do we know the background, the original meaning of the words, the movement of the passage, and the overall, surrounding, and immediate contexts?

We must never use a verse, or verses, to support any view, even if the idea we are supporting is true, unless and until we are sure that what we are quoting is dealing with and supports the position we are attempting to prove.

By using good scholarship to determine the meaning of the words, we can also model before the congregation how to handle the Word of God accurately.

Don't fall into the habit of quoting the Scriptures until you know their meaning. Know your Bible. Strap yourself to your desk until you have dug out the message and know for sure what God is really saying.

∾

TAKING A POSITION
BOTH COURAGE AND WISDOM MUST BE EXERCISED

Give me one hundred preachers who fear nothing but sin and desire nothing but God, and I care not a straw whether they be clergymen or laymen; such alone will shake the gates of hell and set up the kingdom of heaven on earth. —JOHN WESLEY

Sometimes it hurts to take a firm stand. On important issues, people will line up on one side or the other. And many of them feel very strongly about their positions. If you do not agree with them, often you are criticized, verbally attacked, vilified, mocked, avoided, or purposely shunned. And that hurts!

But this goes with the territory. The Scriptures require us to take strong stands on *important* areas of truth. And when we do, we can expect to come into conflict with people on the other side. We see this in the lives of many of God's choice servants. Moses, David, Joshua, Isaiah, Paul, Tyndale, Luther, Calvin, and Jesus Himself had to stand up and be counted. And it often came at great cost. In some cases it cost their very lives. But where would we be today if these men had failed to stand up for the truth?

Now that takes great wisdom and discernment. We must use good judgment to decide what are minor issues on which we can give and what are major truths about which we cannot budge an inch. Too many people have hurt the cause of Christ by being totally inflexible on minor issues, and others have damaged the cause of Christ by failing to stand firm on major points of controversy.

There is no question that we are
to be salt and light in a
crooked, perverse culture.

How do we check ourselves to make sure we are correct before we speak out strongly on disputed issues? First, we must know the Scriptures. Second, we should check our positions with godly leaders in our own church. Third, it is good to talk with church leaders of other sound congregations to make sure that our church has not unintentionally gotten off the main track and sidelined ourselves with wrong conclusions or nonessential matters.

And last, we should be willing to back up, reexamine our stance, and admit any error. If we confirm that our view is correct and that this matter is essential, we should be willing to stand alone, if necessary, despite the numbers who may disagree with us. I'm glad Luther did not budge. And I'm glad Paul was willing to stand face to face even with the great apostle Peter and say, "You are wrong, brother." These men stood firmly against powerful foes and preserved the Gospel for you and me!

MAJORING ON THE MINORS
WE CAN MISS THE REAL ISSUE!

For I resolved to know nothing while I was with you except Jesus Christ and him crucified. —1 CORINTHIANS 2:2

It's easy for pastors and for churches to get involved and spend most of their energy on important but ultimately minor areas. God's Word instructs us to make "the most of every opportunity, because the days are evil" (Ephesians 5:16). The Scriptures speak of our lives as mist that is here for the briefest of periods and then passes off the scene (James 5:14). For that reason, we need to know the difference between the majors and the minors.

It is easy to emphasize the wrong things. Abortion is a godless, evil practice. America was once a much more God-fearing nation than it is now. Gambling can become an addiction and can financially ruin families. These are areas about which we must speak up. The problem is, we can get so wrapped up in these matters that we are known only as "aginners" rather than men and churches who hold up the richness of the Gospel (which alone has the power to change lives). There is no question that we are to be salt and light in a crooked, perverse culture. And we should speak out loudly and clearly in these areas of morality. But if we are not careful, too much of our time and energy can be directed there, and we find that it has been weeks or months since we have confronted a single person with the message of salvation or since we have directed our energy and our messages toward the positive, spiritual growth of the body.

There are many minor areas that must be addressed, but there has to be a proper balance between those concerns and the concern for the clear preaching of the Gospel and the spiritual growth within the congregation.

Churchianity can also become a major. Managing the church can become all-absorbing to the point that there are no new people coming into the church through conversion. We do not find in Scripture any woes pronounced for not attending a church committee meeting, but Paul does say, "Woe to me if I do not preach the gospel!" (1 Cor. 9:16). God certainly must be the one who converts, but He has chosen to use human means. Romans 10:14 says the lost must hear the message. Our tasks are to proclaim the Gospel of Jesus Christ clearly and to build up His body, the church, through the faithful teaching of His Word.

THE TYRANNY OF THE URGENT
THOSE LESS IMPORTANT BUT URGENT DEMANDS UPON US

Until I come, devote yourself to the public reading of Scripture, to preaching and to teaching. Do not neglect your gift, which was given you through a prophetic message when the body of elders laid their hands on you. Be diligent in these matters; give yourself wholly to them, so that everyone may see your progress. —1 TIMOTHY 4:13-15

Today the pastor is expected to be a generalist who knows and does everything in the church. You can see this by the many requests he gets and the problems that find their way to his desk. He is expected to know about current world events, about all the social needs in his area, about how to raise money for the building program, about how to keep the sanctuary temperature at a level that pleases everyone, about how to deal with all sorts of strange behaviors, and about a host of other problems.

Further, he is expected to be Johnny-on-the-spot when any problem occurs, whether it is spiritual, emotional, physical, or affects the building in any way. Personal visits, letters, notes, and phone calls come flooding into his study to make him aware of all sorts of church problems and opportunities for service. Never mind that there are other elders or deacons who could easily handle the need and who may be better trained or more naturally equipped to do so. It is expected that the pastor/teacher must know and do something about these crucial areas. Sometimes even when the janitor has not sufficiently stocked the ladies' restroom with towels or toilet paper, the pastor is reminded of the need.

Trying to show genuine concern and love for his people, he will usually break his neck trying to know and do all that is needed or requested in all of these areas. But this is wrong. His main priority should not be to please the members but to please his Master. His Master has not told him to tend to all of the many perplexities of the modern church. His job, as defined by his Lord, is to spend time in the Word and prayer, so he can equip others to take care of these "urgent" needs. It is a matter of recognizing priorities. God has set the parameters, and 1 Timothy 4 makes abundantly plain what they are.

Our Secretaries
THEY'RE INVALUABLE! BUT WE MUST BE CAREFUL!

Can a man scoop fire in his lap without his clothes being burned?
—PROVERBS 6:27

We have to have them. They do our work. They channel our calls. They protect our schedule. They remind us of our appointments and of areas that need attention. They encourage us when the going gets rough. They work faithfully and many times long hours. If we are smart we will honor them regularly for their unselfish devotion to Christ, to His church, and to our ministry.

If the hours were tallied up, the truth is that we probably spend more waking hours in the office with our secretaries than in our homes with our wives. We probably use more words with them than we do with our wives. They see our better sides, and we see them at their best. Unlike our wives, our secretaries do not see what we look like when we crawl out of bed in the morning, nor witness our failures, crankiness, and sins at home—things we would never intentionally let others see at the office. For many secretaries who do not see the other side of us, we pastors can become heroes; similarly, for many pastors, our secretaries can do no wrong.

We probably spend more waking hours in the office with our secretaries than in our homes with our wives.

Therein lies a terrible temptation that has burned, even destroyed many a pastor. Perhaps things at home are not going just right, or the pastor's marriage relationship has become a bit humdrum. When he gets to the office, romance on some level can begin with his secretary. When that occurs, he is about to be burned! Many a pastor has destroyed his ministry, his family, his church, and even other families by not dealing with his secretary, or for that matter his organist, his pianist, etc., with great caution. This is a tragedy without comparison.

Never be alone behind closed doors with them. Never touch them. Never! Even if you think it is only a goodwill gesture or a reassuring hug. Always look into their eyes when talking with them. Never talk about intimate matters with them. Do not discuss intimate personal problems, hurts, or desires. Never! Never be in an automobile alone with them. Never go to a meeting alone with them. If your mind begins to dwell upon one of them, do whatever is necessary to immediately put it to an end. Go to whatever length, even resigning if it takes that to remove the temptation. Christ made it very plain: Pluck out your eye or cut off your right hand if that is what it takes. The situation can be that serious. Your ministry can be totally destroyed by one mistake in this area. Don't carry fire in your lap. You *will* be burned.

OUR OFFICE DOORS
OPEN? SHUT? DANGEROUS!

The man who wishes to make himself useful in Christ's service must devote all his energies to maintaining the honour of his ministry.
— JOHN CALVIN

It must be obvious that the most important ingredient of the minister's sermon is his character. — S. E. MCNAIR

Privacy and confidentiality in dealing with members and their problems are a must in our society today. As a result, the pastor/elder often finds himself closeted with people. And when this involves someone of the opposite sex, dangers lurk.

When possible we should have some women trained who can counsel other women. In fact, Titus 2:4 talks about this very thing. Older women are to train the younger women how to love their husbands and children. This involves not only training in theory, but also practical instruction.

But, unfortunately, in many situations that is not possible. Either there are no women in the body who are trained or who judge themselves as qualified to provide this help, or in some situations the female counselee will insist upon talking only to the pastor. But certain dangers and liabilities exist when privacy is needed.

First, the situation can have an appearance of evil when a pastor is in a closed session with a woman. Second, a pastor could be falsely accused by the woman, her husband, or someone else of having said or done something improper. And if such an accusation occurs, the pastor has nothing but his word with which to defend himself. Third, occasionally when wives are experiencing marital difficulties with their husbands, they feel lonely and can easily begin to feel an emotional attachment to their pastor. The reverse can also occur. The pastor can begin to develop improper feelings toward the woman he is counseling.

Here is where our subject at hand comes in. Should a pastor ever be alone with a woman behind his closed office door? If not, how does he counsel her if privacy is needed?

Here are a few alternatives: We can leave the door open so our secretaries can be aware of what is being said and done (though this is often not suitable). We can insist upon another pastor sitting in with us. We can require that an adequate-sized window be installed in our office door so everything can be seen by our secretaries. We can ask the counselee to bring a trusted friend. Or we can insist that our wives sit in on the meeting.

The best two options would be qualified women counselors who can do this work or to have the woman counselee bring her own husband, if possible.

Whatever we choose, if our door must be shut when counseling a person of the opposite sex, we had better make certain we have some safeguards in place. Just one single but totally unfounded accusation can destroy our ministries and our congregations, as can one improper word or act if the pastor yields to temptation.

❧

Assuming Too Much
WE'RE NOT THAT PRIVILEGED

A self-serving minister is one of the most loathsome sights in all the world. —Walter J. Chantry

In the small town where I grew up, the local newspaper ran an article about a prominent pastor who was brought to trial for hundreds of past-due parking fines. As he was brought before the judge, he indignantly claimed that as a pastor he should not have to pay any of the fines nor have to pay to park at all. That reasoning and attitude hurt his ministry and harmed the reputation of the other pastors in that locality.

In another church situation a young associate pastor made a reasonable salary but would not live within his means. As a result he often had financial burdens that required special attention by either the other pastors or the deacons. It was an embarrassment for all concerned. It appeared at times that the young man assumed that regardless of the amount of his financial burdens and how they originated, someone or some group must come to his rescue. That was an unfounded and unjustifiable position. Much like the pastor described in the first paragraph, he assumed too much.

As a matter of fact, we are not only never to presume on others, but also to be an example to the flock of the way to live.

Should we pay our parking fines? Yes! In fact, we must live so responsibly that we try to avoid such infractions.

Should we assume that because we are in the ministry all of our personal debts can be unloaded on the church? No. Romans 13:7-8 tells us clearly to pay whatever we owe.

As a matter of fact, we are not only never to presume on others, but also to be an example to the flock of the way to live—in the friends we make, in our response to events, and in managing our finances. We are to have a responsible lifestyle in all respects. Paul says in 1 Thessalonians 4:12 that our "daily life [must] win the respect of outsiders" and that we are not to be "dependent" on anyone. That applies to all believers, preachers included!

Never are we to mooch off others or assume that we are a privileged class. We are to take the lead in giving, not receiving. Our members should be able to point to us and say, "That's the lifestyle I respect and what I want for myself and my family."

꧁

OUR GENUINE NEEDS
WE SHOULDN'T BE ASHAMED TO MAKE THEM KNOWN

Anyone who receives instruction in the word must share all good things with his instructor. —GALATIANS 6:6

The apostle Paul was known as a "tentmaker." He evangelized his known world and on occasion worked with leather goods (probably to make tents) with his own hands. He did this not only to support himself but also to help support some of the gospel coworkers alongside him. Paul did this out of love for people and to avoid letting his financial needs become an offense to anyone. He did not want anyone to have legitimate grounds to charge him as one who preached for money.

It would have been preferable if Paul had always been supported so that he could have devoted all of his waking energy to spreading the Gospel. He, by God's grace, accomplished a tremendous amount for Christ's Kingdom, but he spent valuable time and energy on his trade in order to support himself and others.

There are some pastors today who must be "tentmakers." Perhaps their church is so small and the budget is so pressed that the church cannot adequately support the pastor. Or the pastor may have been saddled with so many expenses such as hospital bills, catastrophes of some type, or family responsibilities that for a period of time he has to earn additional money to supplement his church salary.

If a pastor is serving a congregation that is capable of paying a sufficient wage but does not, the pastor should be up-front and honest with whatever board is responsible for pastoral salaries. Or if unusual expenses (not caused by the pastor's own foolish ways) occur and the pastor is in a financial bind, he owes it to the church to make that need known to the appropriate board. Having to find other forms of occupation would take his time and energy away from the needs of the ministry.

The pastor has only a certain amount of time, energy, and mental toughness, and the ministry deserves it all. I know what I'm talking about because I fell into the trap of trying to always provide for myself, at the expense of my time, attention, and the work of the Gospel. I was too proud in those early years of ministry to let the church bear the load. I wanted to take care of all of it myself, and I fell into a pattern of independence. In retrospect, that was wrong. On occasion the church could not do more, but that should have been the board's decision, not mine alone. Don't make the mistake I did. Make your legitimate needs (but not *greeds*) known.

꿈

Dealing with Panic (Our Own!)
WHEN WE THINK THE SKY IS FALLING!

Do not be anxious about anything, but in everything, by prayer and petition, with thanksgiving, present your requests to God. And the peace of God, which transcends all understanding, will guard your hearts and your minds in Christ Jesus. —Philippians 4:6-7

It doesn't take very long in the ministry to be stricken with panic. It comes in connection with a number of areas. We have to preach, and we're not ready. We are faced with a very serious and complicated problem involving one of our members, and we don't know the proper advice, yet are expected to be the one to provide the appropriate spiritual counsel. We already have a very full schedule, with three full messages to prepare, a wedding, a meeting to chair, along with several other deadlines, and one of our prominent members dies. We must now spend hours consoling the family, working out the funeral arrangements, preparing and then delivering a funeral message that we hope will both lift the spirits of the deceased's family and yet warn the guests of their own mortality and the judgment to come. We are stretched to the limit. And then our wife calls and says she must talk in person, not over the phone!

That is not a once in a lifetime event. Those scenarios come very regularly in the life of the pastor. And they do create panic. Serious panic. What's the answer?

We could resign. But our family must still eat! We could go to bed and tell people we are sick. But we couldn't live with that lie! We could reschedule some events, but then the next week they would pile up and we would probably face the same problem!

The apostle Paul faced panic situations constantly. He tells us of the many deprivations, hardships, and persecutions that constantly faced him. And on top of it all he says that daily he felt the pressure of his concern for all the churches (2 Cor. 11:28). And he had to keep up with quite a number of churches. We only have to be concerned about one!

So what did Paul do? It is evident that he followed Christ's command to take one day at a time and let those troubles be sufficient. He entrusted himself to God's care. He trusted God completely. He presented his prayers and petitions to God, laying his concerns on One who loved him and the church.

Our church is God's church. He loves it supremely. He has not made us into gods, nor has he required any of us to be supermen. There are times when we are so overwhelmed that some things cannot be completed and some things simply cannot be done with the excellence that we would desire. But worry, anxiety, and depression are all sins. Taking one day at a time, one problem at a time, and doing the best we can, committing our problems to God will rest our minds and provide us with the peace we need. The results, left in God's hands, will often surprise us.

CONFUSING THE GOSPEL
THE ONE THING WE MUST MAKE PLAIN

Salvation is found in no one else, for there is no other name under heaven given to men by which we must be saved. —ACTS 4:12

Peter often acted impulsively and sometimes got things wrong. But when he was preaching at Pentecost, he got it right! He cut right through the ignorance, hard-heartedness, and hypocrisy of the Jewish people and stated it in a nutshell: Jesus Christ is the only answer! Neither morality, good deeds, heritage, history, good intentions, nor anything else matters when it comes to the question of salvation. Jesus is the only way to be saved.

Neither morality, good deeds, heritage, history, good intentions, nor anything else matters when it comes to the question of salvation. Jesus is the only way to be saved.

Today there are so many options placed before our pluralistic society. Both well-intentioned people and charlatans are claiming they have the answer. And billions of people are being deluded. Their souls are at risk, and the majority of them are never enlightened about the saving work of Christ. Even in our evangelical churches we can so cloud the Gospel with our attempts to draw crowds and with our desires to compete with those who make people comfortable that we shave the uniqueness off the gospel message.

The Gospel cuts. It is sharp. It is divisive. It does make people uncomfortable. It says there is only one way, that Jesus is *the* way, *the* truth, and *the* life and that there is no hope for anyone outside the work of the God/man, Jesus Christ.

That message will separate us from our family, our neighbors, some of our coworkers, and perhaps even from those in our own denomination. Many will advise us to be more tolerant and non-offensive, to make people comfortable, to not upset the status quo, to preach in such a way that people will feel good about themselves and others. But the truth remains, Jesus is the *only* way!

That must come out in our messages, our conversations, our purpose and mission statements, our church programs, and our lives. If that is not our essential message, we have misunderstood our calling.

Peter was abundantly clear. Many of the Jews rejected his message. But God had others there who would respond, and by the grace of God thousands had their lives transformed. No other message will change lives eternally. The simple, timeless message of the Gospel is the power of God's salvation (Rom. 1:16-17)!

෴

NEGLECTING EXERCISE AND RECREATION
I'M LAZY, STIFF, AND SORE!

For physical training is of some value.   —1 TIMOTHY 4:8

All work and no play can make dull people. That's true about preachers. Not getting sufficient exercise can affect our appearance, endurance, temperament, and productivity. God made our bodies, and what He makes is good. Our bodies are temples of the Holy Spirit, and that alone should cause us to treat them properly. Our service to the Lord takes place through this outer shell, and we must not let our bodies deteriorate. If we do, our service generally becomes poorer.

Should you think that the above biblical phrase has been wrenched from the text, I am aware that Paul goes on to say that though bodily training is of some value, "godliness has value for all things." Obviously, personal holiness should be our primary objective in this life, not our bodies. But that does not mean that the first phrase of the verse is to be ignored and that our bodies are of no consequence.

Our bodies are temples of the Holy Spirit.

How do we take care of our bodies without improperly using the time needed for our souls? It can be a matter as simple as planning. Why not do two things at once? Exercise such as walking can be done while listening to a good message on tape or viewing helpful videos. Perhaps we could double up on some form of physical activity while at the same time providing friendship, fellowship, counseling, accountability, or discipleship for one or more of our members. In fact, to help us maintain a disciplined habit of exercise, it is very helpful to involve other people who will hold us accountable.

Do we want to do great things for the Kingdom? We must not neglect our souls, nor should we neglect our bodies. Both need regular attention in this life.

CHRISTIAN LIBERTY FOR THE PASTOR
ENJOY IT, BUT DON'T LET IT BE AN OFFENSE

"Everything is permissible"—but not everything is beneficial.
"Everything is permissible"—but not everything is constructive.
—1 CORINTHIANS 10:23

Paul's words apply to laymen and pastors alike. In fact, Paul was applying these words not only to the Corinthians, but to himself as well. Paul was a preacher of the Gospel, and he was maintaining that we have a great deal of liberty in regard to things that are neither right nor wrong in and of themselves. Yet there will be times when those things are neither beneficial nor constructive.

In our culture, activities such as movies, drinking alcoholic beverages, wearing jewelry, purchasing something on Sundays, smoking a pipe, etc. can be either right or wrong depending upon a number of factors. These examples are not specifically condemned by the Scriptures, and thus we must apply other criteria. For example, would these matters cause us to sin, or harm our bodies, or cause a brother to stumble, or tempt us to fall into a pattern we could not control? Clearly if those things occurred, then it would be wrong for us to do them. If not, then we have the liberty to enjoy these activities.

But there is another principle for us to consider. As teachers and as examples to the congregation, we will be judged with greater strictness (see, for example, James 3:1). With our position comes greater responsibility. We do want to enjoy the liberty God has given us, and we also want our congregation to enjoy the world He has made for all of us. But at the same time we must be aware that we are being watched very carefully by both the saved and the lost people around us.

What this means is that we can enjoy our Christian liberty, but we must do so very carefully, realizing that we are being watched and tested constantly. Critics of Christianity are continually on the lookout for a pastor who falls into sin (or for that matter, perceived sin), and believers are constantly looking to us as examples. Perhaps the greatest expression of our liberty is for us to freely set aside something that we have freedom to do—for the sake of others.

Our activities and pleasures of this life must be the result of a deliberate, well-thought-out analysis of what we will and will not do. Paul could sum up his life by saying that he would not be mastered by anything (1 Cor. 6:12). If we are at the point where we cannot give up a practice that has brought offense even though we have the liberty to continue in it, then we are being mastered by it. Paul would then say that it is neither permissible nor constructive!

SHACKLES FOR THE PASTOR
DON'T BE NEEDLESSLY BOUND UP

Do not allow what you consider good to be spoken of as evil. For the kingdom of God is not a matter of eating and drinking, but of righteousness, peace and joy in the Holy Spirit, because anyone who serves Christ in this way is pleasing to God and approved by men. Let us therefore make every effort to do what leads to peace and to mutual edification. —ROMANS 14:16-19

There are many stereotypes as to what a pastor is and what he should or should not do. For recreation and just getting away from the daily grind of life, I like to hunt, play golf, and fish, in that order. Most folks would have no problem with my playing golf or fishing, but hunting—well, that's a different story. When people come to my home and observe my trophies of deer, antelope, boar, bear, and mountain lion, a few are perplexed that I could shoot an animal, especially since I am a pastor. Their typical view of a pastor is that a "man of the cloth" is not an outdoorsman. And for some of them, killing an animal is downright wrong. What can I do to keep others from putting me in shackles to the point that I can no longer enjoy those recreational hobbies?

One thing I do is to explain that when I first began hunting deer in our state, it was estimated that we had only about 700 in the entire state. Just to see a deer then was really unusual. Now our Game and Fish Commission estimates that we have a deer herd of approximately 1,000,000. How did that occur? It came about because hunters began to pay for licenses and permits, which helped sustain the Game and Fish Commission, and they in turn began to regulate the hunt. By their control, the herd has grown astronomically, and now there are plenty to go around. So for deer, in one sense, hunters are their very best friends (though some would obviously argue that point).

I also try to explain that since this great increase in numbers of deer has occurred, our state has established the maximum carrying capacity of deer and has concluded that if we do not control them they will eat themselves out of existence and die a miserable death of starvation. The increasing numbers of deer will also present a serious danger on our highways. And unless one is a total vegetarian, we all eat animals that have been raised to be slaughtered. Further, I point out that God has made all things for us to enjoy, as long as it is done in moderation. But I never try to convince them that they must hunt. That could cause them to go against their consciences, and for them it would then be wrong.

Now, if I served in a church where the vast majority of the members were opposed to all forms of hunting, I would have only two choices. Either I would need to move to another congregation or give up hunting until the members were comfortable with my liberty in regard to it. If that were my situation, then I could not exercise my liberty until the consciences of most members changed in this area.

There is so much more to know, and we have only begun to scratch the surface.

Actually the makeup of our congregation is such that the majority of the congregation has no problem regarding hunters. In fact, often when I hunt I use that time to enjoy God's creation with others of our congregation. And through the years it has brought me much closer to quite a few of these men. It has also given me opportunity to spend a week or two in close confines with some lost men whom we have taken with us. That's a great situation. They are a captive audience. And through the years we have seen conversions as a result of those times together.

Christian liberty takes a great deal of sound judgment. But don't be shackled all of your life so that you cannot enjoy God's creation. He made it, and it is good!

ARE WE THE RESIDENT AUTHORITY?
WE DO NOT KNOW IT ALL

A man's pride brings him low, but a man of lowly spirit gains honor.
—PROVERBS 29:23

Without question, we are to know what we are talking about. This requires both formal and private study. It means we either need to own or have access to a good library, and we are to use it regularly. When we step into the pulpit to handle a portion of God's inspired Word or some part of His truth, we had better know what we are talking about. As teachers we will be judged with greater strictness (James 3:1).

Because of that, pride easily creeps in. People refer to us as Bible scholars and often refer biblical, theological, psychological, or sociological questions to us as the resident experts. Often we assure people that if we don't know the answer, at least we know where to find the answer. And so we are set up on a pedestal, with our admiring congregation all around us.

Our pride comes in when we really begin enjoying such accolades and act as if they were deserved. The truth is that while we may have studied in some areas and have developed a fair amount of expertise in certain disciplines, there is so much more to know, and we have only begun to scratch the surface. We must be prepared to say, "You know, I really am not very informed in that area."

Are we afraid that such a statement could ruin our reputation? After all, we guide people's lives in so many areas, and it wouldn't look right if we told them we are ordinary mortals and in some areas are truly uninformed. But actually, admitting our ignorance and showing a bit of humility could help break down some of the barriers that have been erected between us shepherds and the sheep!

WHEN FEAR STRIKES
WE HAVE A SOVEREIGN MASTER

One night the Lord spoke to Paul in a vision: "Do not be afraid; keep on speaking, do not be silent. For I am with you, and no one is going to attack and harm you, because I have many people in this city."
—ACTS 18:9-10

I came to you in weakness and fear, and with much trembling.
—1 CORINTHIANS 2:3

For the minister, fear is an ever-present reality! We must face both the saved and the lost and often declare things they do not want to hear. We must go before our boards and committees on occasions and strongly disagree with them. Individuals must be forced to look squarely at their own lives, sins, and weaknesses and be called on to privately or publicly repent. In some of these situations people leave the church or, in the case of prospects, determine that they want no part of us or our ministries. In some parts of the world, verbal persecution, bodily injury, and even death occur to the faithful ministers of the Word of God.

On top of these possibilities there is the problem of feeling inadequate for the job, recognizing our own inferiority, sins, and ineptness. And when our schedule becomes so crowded that we haven't had time to prepare adequately for a message, fear jumps in with both feet.

Paul, the greatest of the apostles, felt fear. He told the Corinthians that he came to them "in weakness . . . and with much trembling." God had to assure Paul in a dream that no one would attack him so as to harm him, because He had "many people in this city." That was God's way of assuring Paul that He, God, was in charge. And that truth is what we need in large doses from time to time as we conduct our ministries.

God is sovereign. He is the supreme ruler. He knows what is best,

He is powerful enough to bring about what is best, and He loves His church supremely, much more than we do.

Therefore we must do God's work in God's way, declaring God's truth on His terms. That calls for trust—an absolute reliance upon God! The modern church often is afflicted by fear—fear of the members, fear of the world, fear of the unknown, fear of trying to do things God's way. But it is His church, and His Word tells us how to feed His church with His truth and to leave the results in His sovereign hands.

They are strong, loving hands. They are hands that are never defeated. They are hands that can crush an opponent but also can gently cradle a spiritual baby. They are hands that can protect us and can discipline us when needed. They are hands we can trust! Paul could acknowledge his fear. We can also. But Paul immediately placed his trust in the Master of the entire universe.

⟨🐟⟩

TAKING ALL THE BLAME FOR FAILURES
MAYBE WE HAVEN'T SHARED THE LOAD

Our Lord has many weak children in his family, many dull pupils in his school, many raw soldiers in his army, many lame sheep in his flock. Yet he bears with them all, and casts none away. Happy is that Christian who has learned to do likewise with his brethren.

—J. C. RYLE

"He ain't heavy, he's my brother." That picture of a poor, struggling young boy gladly carrying the heavy weight of a tired or suffering brother is a beautiful picture of what a church should be like. Christ instructs us in His Word to carry one another's crushing burdens.

There are going to be times in congregations when we make serious mistakes. We will simply blow it, and our stupidity or bad judgment is hung out there for all to see. That is terribly embarrassing and humbling.

Those times could be when a pastor embarks on a sermon series, a particular program, or an attempt to help a certain member. Then the matter blows up in his face. Since he has initiated the whole thing, and he is alone, he has no one to blame but himself. He has no one to help carry the load and must suffer, isolated to some degree from the congregation.

Perhaps if he had enlisted the wisdom of others he might have been saved from this mistake. But now he is all alone.

But that is not God's design for His church. He anticipates multiple leaderships in His local bodies. He wants us to draw on a number of godly consultants. By doing so, different avenues can be more fully explored and better options selected.

I have been told that for many years a well-known scholar was pastor of a church of 700 people. He began to preach through the book of Hebrews and continued the series for seven years. At the end of those seven years of messages on that one book, his congregation had dwindled to seventy people. No doubt, due to his intensive scholarship, he left no stone unturned in exegeting the text and message of this important New Testament book. But it appears that his judgment about his congregation's ability to stay with him through the study was faulty. Perhaps if his congregation had been blessed with a plurality of leaders who would have been open and honest with him, telling him that he needed to either speed up or end his Hebrews series, the church might have survived and grown. I am sure that after seven years he had a well-informed congregation, but a much smaller one! And one wonders if there was any positive influence on the lost world around him.

Had the pastor regularly counseled with some coleaders, they probably could have jointly chosen a better path.

When joint decisions are made, they are often much better than those made by one person. And when on occasions those decisions are wrong, the pastor does not have to shoulder the entire burden alone. He has others around him to help carry his load.

TAKING CREDIT FOR SUCCESS
PRIDE GOES BEFORE OUR FALL

*No man is weaker than a proud man. For a proud man rests on
nothing.* —RICHARD SIBBES

*God sends no one away empty except those who are full of them-
selves.* —D. L. MOODY

God will not go forth with that man who marches in his own strength.
—C. H. SPURGEON

*If we think we can do anything of ourselves, all we shall get from God
is the opportunity to try.* —C. H. SPURGEON

A pastor I served with for a number of years told me about his first
pastorate as an associate in a small-town church. The senior pastor
had been there for many years. And as the community grew so did
the church, both in numbers and reputation. He told me that on occasions he would be in an automobile with the senior pastor, who loved
to park in front of the massive church plant, swelled up with pride.
He would then explain that what they were admiring was something
that he, the senior pastor, had built over a number of years. That
senior pastor was proud of his accomplishments and was continually
drawing attention to himself as the grand builder of that church.

Obviously, that is an extreme example. And to the young associate it was thoroughly disgusting. I can imagine how God viewed it.
Most of us would never be so overt so as to openly flout our egos and
pride. But that attitude can certainly be hidden in the dark recesses of
our own corrupt hearts.

God despises pride. Pride usually leads into a terrible fall.
Only Satan can convince us that we, by our own strength, have
accomplished anything good spiritually. If through our talents,
gifts, and opportunities anything spiritually good has been accomplished, we must always give God the glory. From whom did we

secure our talents? Who has ultimately arranged our opportunities? Who is the only One who can open men's hearts? Who unstops men's spiritual ears? Who is the One who grants repentance and faith? It is God alone! He is the sovereign One, both in the physical and spiritual realms.

We have absolutely no power to get into men's hearts and change them. They are dead spiritually and cannot lift a finger toward God's mercy and grace. He must therefore be the One who comes to sinners, granting to them undeserved mercy. And if He happens to plant them within our ministry, He, not we, must receive all the glory. We are simply caretakers of their souls for a brief period of time. They are His creation, His sheep, His called-out ones, and we are merely undershepherds, serving under the great Shepherd of their (and our) souls.

Why can't we realize this? It is probably because of imbedded human conceit. Our fallen natures want us to think we are something, but the truth is that we are nothing apart from Christ!

To God alone belongs the glory in His church now and forever!

LITIGATION

DOCUMENTATION, CONFIDENTIALITY, CARE, AND PROTECTION—THE ONLY WAY FOR THE MODERN PASTOR TO CONDUCT HIS MINISTRY

Wisdom in ruling is justice; wisdom in speech is discretion; wisdom in conduct is prudence; wisdom in evaluation is discernment.
—GEORGE SEEVERS

We live in a very litigious society. People will sue others for practically anything and everything. Lawyers are now advertising their specialties—automobile accidents, long-haul truck claims, products liability, class action suits, divorces. Some even specialize in suing certain companies or regarding very specific activities. Pastors and churches are no longer exempt but have become fair game. And we are becoming increasingly vulnerable in a number of ways.

As we deal with members' marital disputes, we can be sued by either party. As we counsel people suffering from depression we are at risk if one of them commits suicide. As we lead our congregation in discipline cases we open ourselves to possible litigation. Church leaders can be sued over what is perceived as improperly handling church funds. The Gospel can separate families, and the church and its leaders can be sued claiming a form of cultish mind control. Parents can sue us over alleged child molestation in our church programs, classes, or nurseries. The possibilities are endless. And it is sad to say, in some cases the church and its workers have been found guilty.

What can we do in the face of such tremendous vulnerability? There are at least five methods that can provide some measure of protection for us and our boards.

- We must document meetings, facts, figures, and conversations. Judges look dimly on vague memories and hearsay. All financial matters must have solid documentation with adequate paper trails. Confidential counseling discussions should be documented and, if possible, tape recorded (though in many instances that will neither be allowed nor preferable).
- We are often put in the position of complete trust. That involves great exposure with regard to confidentiality. If not properly maintained, a breach of trust or libel litigation can result. We therefore must be very careful in entering into confidential discussions because they may involve information that must come to light. But if we do, and when it is appropriate for such discussions to take place, we must live up to our commitments. If we cannot make such a promise, we should encourage the counselee to reconsider the confidentiality issue or to go elsewhere.
- Great care must be taken when hiring people and when accepting volunteers for the church. Careful screening and background checks should be made of those whom we

choose to be pastors, board members, Sunday school supervisors and teachers, ministry directors, nursery workers, and youth pastors. Their employee files must be documented. Pertinent questions must be asked on the screening forms. Church practices and requirements must be stressed before anyone is hired. Those not meeting the qualifications must be gently turned down.

• Adequate liability insurance for all possible exposures should be purchased. Those coverages should include protection for all the activities of the church. Basic coverage plus umbrella liability coverage with high limits should be secured. The exposures protected against should include officers' and directors' liability, counseling liability, sexual molestation coverage, property damage liability, personal and physical injury liability, employee grievance liability, and others. We should ask our agents to explain to us all of the available protection and secure quotations on the broadest possible coverages. Financial considerations will determine just how much we purchase, but we need to be informed as to the possible risks and available protection from these risks. Suits against us may be dismissed or won by us, but the expenses to defend ourselves can be enormous. By securing liability coverage the insurance company will defend us at their cost, thus protecting us in more than one way. Often they will use some of the very best attorneys, and many times that will aid dramatically in our defense.

• It is also important that we attend classes and seminars that deal with legal matters. Knowledge gained from these sources may help prevent situations from occurring that would involve us in litigation.

With so many people today looking for ways to get some easy money, and with the abundance of attorneys, some of whom are unscrupulous, we must protect ourselves in every legal and moral way possible. Christ wants us to be as innocent as doves, but He also instructs us to be as wise as serpents. Protecting ourselves and our flocks in these ways is a means of exercising that wisdom.

FOR ADDITIONAL STUDY

General Warnings

Woes to false teachers: Matthew 23:1-39.

Self-righteousness: Luke 16:14-15; Luke 18:9-14.

False shepherds: John 10:1-13; 2 Peter 2:1—3:18.

False elders: Acts 20:25-31.

Judaizers: Galatians 1—6; Philippians 3:1-2, 17-21.

False judgments: Colossians 2:16-23.

Pastoral instructions: 1 Timothy 1—6; 2 Timothy 1—3; Titus 1—3.

Teachers: James 1:19-27; James 3:1-18.

Living as examples: 1 Peter 5:1-4.

Deceivers: 2 John 7-11.

Those who love to be preeminent: 3 John 9-10.

Godless men: Jude 3-22.

Churches in sin: 1 Corinthians 5:1—6:20; Revelation 2:1—3:22.

Section Ten

MISCELLANEOUS

WHY NOT FEMALE PASTORS?
A BIBLICAL IMPOSSIBILITY

Now the overseer must be . . . the husband of but one wife.
—1 TIMOTHY 3:2

Sincerity, talent, and developing a following are not the only tests of a ministry. More important factors are the biblical qualifications and God's design for the ministry. And His plan for the ministry is that the pastor be a male. First Timothy 3:2 and Titus 1:6 make that so clear that one has to use some very faulty hermeneutics to allow women to take part in the office of pastor/elder.

Yet today we are losing in the battle to obey God in this critical area. More and more seminaries, denominations, and churches are recognizing and accepting females into the ministry. And those of us who insist it is wrong are often characterized as old-fashioned, male chauvinists who are out of touch with present-day realities. We are also told that we are stifling important and useful gifts and abilities given to women.

There is no question that many women are very godly, are often extremely good Bible students, know how to lead others, possess excellent reputations, have good management and people skills, and can explain the Scriptures better than many men. We must acknowledge that very clearly. In fact, in many churches today the women are the real servants. We salute them and thank God for them.

Yet the truth still remains: Women are not called to be pastors. There is no way a woman can become "the husband of but one wife." God has never called a woman to pastor a church, and He never will. I can say that unequivocally because His Word says that it should not occur, that it is not God's design for the church. Men are to be the leaders. That is consistent with God's order in all of His creation. He has chosen men to be the leaders over creation, in the home, and in the church.

But what about those situations where female pastors seem to be having tremendous success in the ministry? Or what about those ministries where no men step forward and as a result the women are forced to carry on the work of ministry? Two answers: First, it is God's church, and He is the one who establishes the rules. And His rules simply do not allow female leadership. That does not mean that God cannot bring good out of something He disagrees with. Christ should not have been crucified, yet God brought eternal good out of Christ's sacrifice.

And second, our attempts to help out God's plan can be very perilous. Consider the Old Testament man who simply touched the ark of the covenant to keep it from falling off the cart. God killed him. He was trying to do God's work, but not the way God wanted it done. What he did appeared very reasonable, but God looked upon it differently. He had made it plain that the ark should not be touched by ordinary men.

He has chosen men to be the leaders over creation, in the home, and in the church.

I am not saying that God will eventually kill women preachers. God undoubtedly appreciates women who are willing to serve, but at the same time he must be appalled and angered that we try to explain away His clear Word, which says that only men are to occupy the position of pastor/elder. In many ways women may do a better job than some men, but that's not the test. The test is God's requirements, and His Word is extremely clear.

Women can serve in almost any other area. They can teach groups of women or children (three-fourths of the world's population). The two things they cannot do are to be pastors or to have authority over and teach men. Other than those areas, they have many, many ministry opportunities. And we thank God for those who serve ably in the proper capacity.

THE SENIOR PASTOR

MAYBE "PREACHING PASTOR," OR "PASTOR/TEACHER," OR BETTER STILL, "ONE OF THE PREACHING PASTORS"

The elders who direct the affairs of the church well are worthy of double honor, especially those whose work is preaching and teaching.
—1 TIMOTHY 5:17

Many of the seminary graduates I have met finish their coursework and embark on the path of trying to become the senior pastor of a local church. It seems that many seminaries breed that thought into them. But there are at least two serious problems with that view. First, it may help create a bit of pride to elevate one to such a position so quickly. But more important, it is unbiblical.

There is no such position in the Scriptures. In all the passages dealing with elders/pastors they are always spoken of in the plural, and there is no rank mentioned such as senior pastor, assistant pastor, associate pastor, etc. The Scriptures make it very plain that in a local church there should be a plurality of pastors. There is a distinction, as in 1 Timothy 5:17 above, but the only difference is that some of the elders/pastors earn their living by preaching/teaching and other elders/pastors must hold down secular employment.

It is plain in Scripture that some people are more gifted in certain areas such as preaching, teaching, caring, or administration. And when one is more gifted and fruitful in one of these areas he should serve predominantly in that particular way. For example, in a five-member staff, perhaps two or three will excel in the public proclamation of the Word. While the others should be given the opportunity to grow in their preaching ability, those who excel should be the ones who are predominantly up front. But the others are not secondary pastors or lower-level pastors.

Scripture nowhere speaks of a "Senior Pastor." Some men, such as James (in Jerusalem in the first century), may have occupied a more public role than the other pastors/elders. To be truly biblical there are to be multiple pastors/elders in a local church who all take on a shepherding/pastoral role, provided of course that they all meet the qualifications of an elder, including being apt to teach. And they should each be equally respected, loved, followed, and disciplined if needed (1 Timothy 5:20).

The title given to the position I occupied in my last pastorate was "Executive Pastor." It was given to me to help define my particular role within our pastoral staff. That title, also, is not a biblical term. I don't mean to be legalistic at this point, but I would have preferred that all of us had just been called "pastors" or "elders."

THE PASTOR AND THE IRS

WE MUST KNOW THE RULES AND PLAY BY THEM

So much has been given to me, I have no time to ponder over that which has been denied.   —HELEN KELLER

It seems everyone wants to complain about the IRS. Today the agency is under both serious scrutiny and strong congressional and public criticism. Yet, for the pastor the IRS has provided some wonderful ways to save on taxes. Our attitude, therefore, should be both gratitude and complete compliance. But more importantly, we should obey their rules because God instructs us to do so (Rom. 13:1-7).

Even the Social Security system allows us to be exempt from its taxes, should we desire and appropriately complete the forms on time. To claim this exemption, though, we must sign a statement that for conscience's sake we are opposed to paying taxes. I fear that many pastors have signed the form to get out of Social Security payments and have lied about their consciences. That is a very regrettable matter.

But back to the IRS. Part of our wonderful tax break involves the housing allowance given to us by our church. Without trying to get into all the specifics, with the exceptions of money spent on food and, by some, maid service, our housing allowance is exempt from federal income taxes (and in some states, exempt from state income tax).

There are also other substantial deductions. The property taxes we pay on our homes and the interest we pay on our mortgages can become a double deduction. We can include them in the housing allowance figure on which there is no income tax due. We can also include them in our own personal deductible expenses. The combined effect is that the minister can significantly reduce his taxes over what the layman has to pay. That is a wonderfully generous gesture on the part of our government toward pastors.

Then there is a little known deduction that is quite complex to explain. It involves those pastors who have elected to come under a SEP IRA. As ministers, for income tax purposes we are considered a common employee. But as regards Social Security we are viewed as self-employed, and our tax is called self-employment tax. As a self-employed person we should list our housing allowance on the self-employment tax form as income and pay 15.3% of that amount to the Social Security Fund. But we can then also use the amount of our housing allowance to figure the maximum we can contribute to our SEP IRA, which in turn reduces our overall income tax liability. I am not a tax expert, and this explanation may not be clear. Bring this matter up to your tax adviser. It can provide a legitimate way to reduce your taxes.

Pastors who have retired from a denominational church and are covered by their denomination's annuity program may continue to claim a housing allowance on money coming out of the church-sponsored fund. Discuss this matter carefully with your tax adviser to make certain that you qualify.

There are a number of good booklets written specifically about the pastor and his taxes. Each pastor needs to purchase an updated version annually. Certain things about how to handle reimbursable expenses, auto allowances, and other pertinent areas will usually be covered.

The general rule for the pastor in connection with taxes is to be honest, open, and on time. That's what all citizens should do, but as pastors we must set the example. We must protect our reputation, and we should cheerfully cooperate with the government. We are commanded in the Word of God to willingly support those whom God has put in authority over us. And those of us in this country should do so out of gratitude—gratitude toward God for allowing us to live in a free and prosperous nation, and gratitude toward the government for the generous ways in which the IRS treats us as pastors.

ONE-ISSUE CHURCHES
TUNNEL VISION

My observations have led me to the belief that many, perhaps most, of the activities engaged in by the average church do not contribute in any way to the accomplishing of the true work of Christ on earth. I hope I am wrong, but I am afraid I am right.   —A. W. TOZER

As I sit here at my computer and survey the landscape of churches in my area as well as other churches across America, I identify several churches based on the one issue for which they are known. One seems to be concerned primarily about the *King James* translation, one about so-called miracles, one about God and America, one about great social issues, one about soup kitchens, one about sovereign grace, one about theonomy, one about eldership, one about church discipline, and one about positive thinking. Some of these areas are clearly biblical and are important areas about which to be concerned. But they are not the only matters with which God is concerned.

I don't want to be so harsh that I leave the impression that all of their teaching, energy, and concern is devoted to that one issue. But from a distance it appears that their primary focus is that one issue.

That is not the reputation we should seek to have. Our concern should be the whole counsel of God, which includes the Gospel, the truths of the Word of God, morality, the sovereignty of God, the plight of man, genuine social concerns, and other clearly biblical themes. In other words, the Scriptures, when properly taught, will balance out all of these areas. We are to let the Word of God speak through us by seeking diligently to make scriptural truth relevant to the immediate needs around us.

God knows the myriad of needs among mankind, and His message is intended to meet all of those needs adequately. When our views become warped to the point that we are one-issue Christians, we are out of balance and we present God's message in a lopsided manner.

The Bible speaks to the whole man and to the many needs of society. Its truths work when people obey them. Our responsibility is to get all of God's message out to men. The Holy Spirit will balance those truths in the lives of God's people.

FOR ADDITIONAL STUDY

The Description and Work of the Watchman, Workman, Shepherd, Bishop, Overseer, Minister, Pastor, Elder

Ezekiel 33:1-33	Philippians 2:19-24	Hebrews 13:7, 17
John 10:1-18	Philippians 3:1-4	1 Peter 5:1-9
Acts 20:17-38	Colossians 2:1-12	2 Peter 2:1—3:9
1 Corinthians 1:10—4:21	1 Thessalonians 2:1-12	1 John 2:18-19
2 Corinthians 2:1—13:10	1 Thessalonians 3:1-5	2 John 7-11
Galatians 1:6-24	2 Thessalonians 3:1-15	3 John 9-10
Ephesians 3:1-13	1 Timothy 1—6	Jude 3-23
Ephesians 4:11-16	2 Timothy 1—3	Revelation 1:1—3:22
Philippians 1:12-26	Titus 1—3	

APPENDICES

Appendix I
PASTOR'S SELF-EVALUATION QUESTIONNAIRE

By Tim Keller and David Powlison

FROM *THE JOURNAL OF BIBLICAL COUNSELING*, VOL. XII, NO. 1, FALL 1993. USED BY PERMISSION.

(Dr. Keller is pastor of Redeemer Presbyterian Church in New York City and teaches Practical Theology at Westminster Theological Seminary. Dr. Powlison is the editor of *The Journal of Biblical Counseling* and is also a professor at Westminster Theological Seminary.)

"Pay close attention both to yourself and to your teaching; persevere in these things; for as you do this you will save both yourself and those who hear you." (I Timothy 4:16)

The questions that follow help you to pay close attention to yourself and to your teaching. The purpose is to bless you and those you seek to love and serve. For the vast majority of readers, it will help you set a positive, personal agenda for growth as God's instrument. The Great Shepherd of the sheep will by His grace continue to develop you in His image. Conduct your self-evaluation in the light of His love.

Perhaps for a few readers it will prove to be a pass-fail test for your current ministry. Perhaps God has not given you certain gifts. Perhaps you are walking in some disqualifying pattern of sin. Even in these cases the questionnaire serves a positive purpose. The Lord has another place for those gifts that He has given you. The Lord has a way of repentance and renewal for sins that sabotage pastoral integrity and effectiveness. Remember the grace of the gospel.

So set your heart on Christ, on His gospel of mercy, on His high call, on His abounding riches of grace, on His honor in your life and His church. Here are some suggestions on how to profit from this study.

Read the questions carefully. The questions are posed first, followed by work-sheets. The questions range widely over the pastor's role. If you are not a pastor, you can still profit. Ignore the questions that do not apply to your situation.

Think hard. Answer each question honestly after taking time to ponder. Set aside a day or several evenings to reflect on your life and ministry. Wherever possible give concrete examples of fruitfulness or failure, of growth or struggle.

Pray. Pray for wisdom to know God and yourself better. Pray for wisdom to serve God more effectively. Pray to know yourself before the eyes of the God who is both light and love.

Seek counsel from others. Many of the questions are difficult to answer about yourself. This self-evaluation questionnaire will be most useful when you combine it with feedback from others. Ask other leaders, friends, spouse, coworkers on a ministry team, and so forth.

Plan. The work-sheets will guide you in practical planning.

Acknowledge that others have gifts that complement yours. The second half of the questionnaire deals with pastoral skills. You may have limitations which God covers by providing others on the pastoral team with complementary gifts. In acknowledging personal weaknesses, ask yourself whether or not your pastoral team as a whole is covering all the bases.

Remember, the goal of this self-evaluation is to guide you in the path of growing holiness and growing pastoral skill. The questions are divided into these two major sections: personal holiness and pastoral skills. Effective ministers demonstrate holiness by humility, love, integrity and spirituality. Effective ministers are skilled in nurture, communication, leadership and mission.

Under each category you will find several questions. Notice that each question is two-sided. This captures that you fail either by omission or by commission. For example, biblical love is neither careless detachment from others nor obsession with others. You will likely find that you tend towards one side of each question. Let the questions stimulate you to ask further questions. They are not exhaustive. Some will apply to you; some won't.

Part I. Personal Qualifications of Effective Ministers: Holiness

A. Humility

1. Do you acknowledge your limitations and needs out of confidence in Christ's gracious power?

Are you honest enough? Do you demonstrate a willingness to admit your limits, mistakes, sins and weaknesses? Are you defensive, guarded, hypersensitive? Do you model that the Christian life is the open life? Do you demonstrate that the Christian life is a work in process rather than a completed product? Do you deal forthrightly with the common temptations you face: anger, anxiety, escapism, love of pleasure, self-love, materialism, perfectionism, and the like?

Are you too open? Do you wear your heart on your sleeve, indulging and wallowing in your limits, mistakes, sins and weaknesses? Are you morbidly or 'exhibitionistically' confessional? Or have you learned to speak of your weaknesses in ways that (1) point to your confidence in Christ, (2) genuinely seek help from people who can help, and (3) edify others?

2. Do you demonstrate a flexible spirit out of confidence in God's control over all things, God's authority over you, and God's presence with you?

Are you flexible enough? Do you adapt faithfully, flexibly and creatively to the unexpected? Do you value and encourage the ideas and gifts of others? Do you insist on your own way, whether forcefully or through subtle manipulation? Do you exemplify confidence in the sovereign control of God down to the details of life? Are you caught up in the various aggressions and fears produced by a drive to ensure your own control? Are you willing to try things experimentally and then reevaluate and make changes? Are you evidently a learner?

Are you too flexible? Do you bend too much? Do you blow in the wind of others' opinions and get overwhelmed by people's demands and agendas? Do you compromise, under-assert, seek to please, fail to push things that need to be pushed? Do you let people or circumstances control you rather than the Lord?

B. Love

1. Do you have a positive approach to people because of confidence in the power and hope of the Gospel of Jesus Christ?

Do you give grace to others? Do you love and encourage persons, even when under stress or in the face of an attack? Do you exhibit core biblical virtues: love for enemies, gentleness with opponents, patience with people and circumstances when undergoing trial or suffering? Are you able to confront the failings of others—to discipline your children, to admonish wanderers, to conduct church discipline—in a way that is not punitive, irritable, or censorious but breathes the invitations of God's grace? Can you say hard things lovingly? Is your "speaking the truth" harsh, opinionated, idiosyncratic? Do you create problems by making mountains out of molehills? Do you contribute to destructive conflict or to peacemaking?

Are you too tolerant? Are you naively optimistic about people? Do you massage people's egos with praise and "unconditional positive regard"? Is your "love" limp and truthless? Do you whitewash or minimize problems rather than tackle them? Because of biblical love are you willing to enter into constructive conflict? Are you a peace-lover and conflict-avoider rather than a peacemaker?

2. Do you show a servant's heart to people because you are first and foremost a servant of the Lord?

Do you serve willingly? Do you serve yourself or others primarily? Do you truly serve the well-being of others and shepherd them under the Lord? Do you strive for personal glory either aggressively (compulsively driven "on an ego trip") or passively (preoccupied with your "low self-esteem")? Do you manifest the combination of forcefulness and sensitivity, commitment and flexibility, which characterizes servants of the Lord's glory? Do you lord it over other people? Do you resist or avoid serving and loving others?

Do you serve compulsively? Do you serve other people slavishly, kowtowing to their demands, expectations, and whims? Do you let others lord it over you? Are you confused about what it means to serve and love others? Do you know how to say "No" realistically, firmly and graciously? Do you regularly rest and lay aside your work?

C. Integrity

1. Are you responsible to God first and foremost?

Are you irresponsible? Do you follow through on convictions and commitments? Do you speak the truth firmly, confidently, faithfully? Do you "trim" the truth or waffle on your commitments because of convenience or social pressures? Do you fail to demand of yourself and others things that God demands? Do you follow your impulses, moods, and feelings? Are you walking in the grip of a sin: e.g., greed, lust, outbursts of anger, fear of man, drunkenness, pride?

Are you overly demanding? Do you behave in a rigid manner? Do you sledgehammer people because of your commitment to principle? Are you legalistic in your commitments and nit-picking in your convictions? Do you major in minors? Do you make demands of yourself and others which God does not make?

2. Do you demonstrate a disciplined lifestyle under the Lordship of Jesus?

Are you undisciplined? Is your visible life and behavior disciplined, consistent and attractive? Do you manifest the joy, humility, and winsomeness of wisdom and holiness? Would people want to imitate what they see of your faith, your faithfulness, your character? What would people see if they could tag along with you for a week? Do you work diligently or are you lazy?

Are you too rigid? Are you too disciplined, organized, "perfect" on the outside? Does your visible example actually discourage or intimidate people? Are you in effect playing the role of "pastor" or "mature Christian"? Is your visible discipline a mask for hypocrisy, a cover for ignorance of yourself or a denial of a deviant inner life? Are you humbled by conscious awareness that you fight the common besetting temptations of every human heart: pride, fear of man, attachment to money, sexual lust, preoccupation with your own performance, control, judgmentalism, love of various pleasures, and the like? Do you have an active sense of humor? Do you take time to rest or are you consumed with anxious toil?

3. Are your family commitments a proper priority under the Lord?

Do you give yourself to your family? Are you over-committed to your ministry and under-committed to your family? Do you love your family in such a way that they willingly become committed to your ministry and really stand with and behind you? Are they being sacrificed to "ministry"? Are they being dragged along behind you? Do you give to them significantly, substantially, willingly?

Are you over-involved in your family? Are you over-committed to your family so that they provide an improper refuge, distraction and excuse to avoid ministry? Is family life an excuse for selfishness?

D. Spirituality

1. Do you demonstrate personal piety and vigor in your relationship with God?

Is your piety genuine? Is your communion with God rich and growing? Is your personal prayer life both spontaneous and disciplined or are you mostly a public pray-er? Do you apply the Bible searchingly and encouragingly to yourself or only to your hearers? Do you praise, enjoy and thank God with heartfelt integrity? Do you know God, rely on God, seek God, praise God genuinely? What does Christ mean in your life on a day-in, day-out basis? Are you signifi cantly prayer-less, Bible-less, praise-less, God-less, Christ-less?

Are you 'pietistic'? Do you escape into pious clichés and misuse the spiritual disciplines? Do you use "I'll pray about it" or "I need to study the Bible" in order to avoid problems for which you feel inadequate? Do you pray too much (Matthew 6:7) or self-centeredly (James 4:3) because you do not know God very well? Is your Bible, praise and prayer life a hypocritical diversion in a life far from God?

2. *Do you demonstrate faithfulness to the Bible and sound doctrines?*
Are you biblically and theologically careful? Are you orthodox, faithful to the whole counsel of God? Do you have clear, definite, and thought-out biblical positions on the central issues of life? Do you have theological quirks or hobby-horses which upset the balance of truth? Do you articulate core biblical truth clearly and consistently, with a working feel for its personal and pastoral application? Are you ignorant? Fuzzy? In error? Unbalanced?

Are you a theological nit-picker? Are your theological convictions abstract, theoretical, and scholastic? Are you narrowly dogmatic, combative, critical, reductionistic, overly precise in your interpretations and applications of Scripture? Are you simplistic or superficial in your understanding of contemporary life and of human nature? Do you recognize the broad range of questions on which Scripture bears? Do you recognize the many variables which influence the application of Scripture to particular situations?

Part II. Functional Qualifications of Effective Ministers: Pastoral Skill

A. Nurture

1. *Do you show involved caring that comes from genuine love in Christ for your brothers and sisters?*
Do you involve yourself with the needs of others? Do you keep people at a distance? Are you able to develop relationships of honesty and trust through which you can comfort and challenge persons? Are you approachable? Do you create frequent conflict? Do you approach people warmly? Do you communicate care for people in ways they can sense?

Do you become overly absorbed in people? Do you become overly involved with people, caring too much because of a desire to

be liked or a savior-complex or a fear of failure? Do you seek relationships as an end in themselves rather than as a component of pastoring people unto godliness?

2. Do you counsel people the Lord's way?

Do you counsel biblically? Are you skilled in helping people
respond to and solve personal problems using biblical principles? Do
you counsel biblically both informally and formally? Do you use
unbiblical conceptual categories and methods? Is what you say in
your office congruent both with what you say in the pulpit and with
how you yourself live? Do you get involved constructively with trou-
bled people, or do you disdain them, refer them, avoid them? Are
individuals encouraged in godliness, amid their sufferings and sins,
through your personal ministry?

Do you go overboard on counseling? Do you become overly centered on problem people and focus on one-on-one remedial counseling to the detriment of more positive, preventive, building-up and
corporate aspects of the ministry? Do you tend to turn the church into
a counseling center or therapy group?

*3. Do you discipline others into maturity in Christ and use of their
gifts?*

Do you help others productively serve the Lord? Do you demonstrate skills in nurturing growth in grace in individuals and in developing their gifts? Does your ministry have a positive, equipping
thrust to it? Do you develop leaders and team ministries?

Do you focus too much on activism and productivity? Does your
focus on gifts and discipleship have an elitist flavor? Are Christians
with minimal gifts and energies neglected? Are there certain kinds of
gifts which you recognize and encourage to the neglect of other kinds
of gifts? Do you tend to move only with the movers?

*4. Do you give yourself to discipline and to patrolling the boundaries
of the church which God bought with His own blood?*

Do you protect Christ's honor in the church? Are you committed
to church discipline? Are you able to confront winsomely and per-

sistently? Do you recognize the limits of the edification ministries of counseling, care and discipling? Do you stand courageously against real errors and falsehoods which encroach into the body of Christ that you shepherd? Are you realistic that the ministry is a savor both of life and death? Do you try to be so positive that you cannot be properly and biblically negative?

Are you over-absorbed in border patrol? Do you demonstrate a nit-picking, sectarian, vigilante spirit? Are you uncompassionate of people's failings, negativistic rather than upbuilding? Do you create in others a fear of failure and a fear of being found wrong, rather than creating love for ongoing growth in the Lord and love for ever-deepening truth?

B. Communication

1. Do you preach the whole counsel of God?

Are you preaching and teaching the Word of God? Are you skillful in expounding the Word of God publicly so that people are convicted, encouraged, and edified? Do you use the pulpit effectively? Do you downplay the importance of the pulpit and teaching in your attitudes, practice, and theory of ministry? Is what you say in the pulpit congruent both with what you say in your office and with how you yourself live? Do you take adequate time and work hard at preparation, or are you casual and presumptuous?

Are you overly absorbed in your pulpit? Are you overly concerned with pulpit ministry to the detriment of other aspects of pastoral care? Does pride puff you up or does the fear of men tie you in knots? Do you envision yourself as a "pulpiteer," to the harm of reaching people where they live? Do you take too much time to prepare for public ministry because of perfectionism, self-trust, or fear?

2. Do you provide education for God's many kinds of people?

Do you educate all? Are you skilled in identifying Christian Education needs and in helping people learn? Does your philosophy of Christian Education reach all age groups and all different kinds of needs? Is biblical and doctrinal knowledge undervalued? Do you tend to ignore, despise, or belittle the educational needs of certain kinds of people? Does your approach to Christian Education effectively combine truth and practice?

Do you overeducate? Do you tend to turn your church into a school? Is education and factual or doctrinal knowledge overvalued in comparison with other aspects of the Christian life? Is the teacher-pupil role the dominant one in the church or only one role among many?

3. Do you lead others to worship the Lord?

Do you lead others to worship God in truth? Do you lead people into the presence of God? Is your worship perfunctory and rote? Do you yourself worship God as you lead, or does worship become a performance and task? Do you undervalue worship, viewing it only as a glorified warm-up for the message?

Are you overly absorbed in worship? Do you over-emphasize the "worship experience" to the detriment of truth and the other aspects of church life? Are you overly subjective, gauging the Christian life by emotions and sentiment? Do you use words, music, and staging to manipulate experience? Is God at the center of your worship or do you worship the worship?

C. Leadership

1. Do you lead God's people into effective work together?

Do you lead groups of people well? Do you help groups develop a biblical vision, and do you motivate them towards biblical goals? Are you confused about what the goals of groups should be? Are you overly absorbed either in personal one-on-one work with people or in impersonal programs and public ministry? Do you function constructively in groups, or do you hamper and divert groups from achieving God's ends? Do you value groups and encourage them to take on significant responsibilities?

Are you overly absorbed in groups? Do you tend to see groups, committees, and task forces as a panacea or a substitute for other aspects of ministry? Does a task orientation sabotage other biblical goals such as prayer, worship, caring, and counseling?

2. Do you administer well, creating a church that is wise in its stewardship?

Are you a good administrator? Are you skilled in using time, money, and people efficiently to achieve biblical goals in the church? Do you neglect or despise administration?

Are you overly absorbed in administration? Do you tend to over-administer or retreat to administrative tasks because they are easier or are the squeaky wheel?

3. Do you mediate fellowship among God's people?

Do you help people come together? Are you skilled in stimulating the congregation to mutual ministry in love? Does your ministry create one-anothering opportunities and activities among God's people? Do you enhance a family atmosphere in the church? Are you able to teach people how to make significant friendships through your teaching, manner, and example?

Are you overly absorbed with the church's social life? Are you so oriented towards "fellowship and family feeling" that the church's fellowship with God and orientation to mission are lost?

4. Do you create cooperative and team ministry within the church and between churches that honor Christ?

Are you a team player? Do you work well as part of a ministry or pastoral team, or do you always insist on leading (in overt or covert ways)? Do you tend to stake out turf? Is your leadership based on true biblical wisdom or on personal drive, clerical status, and political savvy? Do you build unity and mutual respect among different parts of the body of Christ? Can you cooperate with other evangelical churches and pastors, or do you have sectarian instincts? Are you committed in practical ways to see the work of the local congregation as part of the larger work of Christ? Are you too independent and not enough of a "churchman"?

Do you allow the team to shield you from the front lines of ministry? Do you shirk leadership responsibilities out of diffidence or laziness and seek to embed yourself safely within a niche? Do you put your attention too much into the work of presbyteries, synods, general assemblies, conferences, associations, conventions, ministeriums, school boards and the like? Are you a politician and too much a "churchman" rather than a pastor?

D. Mission

1. Do you evangelize those outside of Jesus Christ?

Are you active in evangelism? Are you skilled both in effectively sharing the gospel and in leading the church in outreach? Are you committed in theory and personal practice to evangelize the lost? Do you believe with all your heart that people without Christ remain under the wrath of God? Do you neglect evangelism out of ignorance, love of comfort, fear, prejudice, bad experiences? Do you lead your people to support worldwide missionary efforts?

Are you overly committed to evangelism? Do you overemphasize evangelism or one evangelistic technique to the detriment of the church's overall ministry? Do you create ministry activists rather than godly people? Do you play a numbers game with evangelism? Do your evangelistic methods hold the message of salvation in Christ in proper balance with God's sovereignty in grace and with the call for us to demonstrate genuine love for each other and the lost? Are missionaries idolized as a higher species of Christian?

2. Do you show social concern for the many needs of people that God desires to address?

Do you care for the whole person? Are you skilled in applying the resources of the church to the social and material needs of mankind? Do you value diaconal work and the mercy gifts? Do you believe that the gospel addresses the whole man, or do you drift towards a gospel that is a bare verbal message? Do you care in practical ways for justice, or do you tacitly accept the status quo? Can you identify the social needs of your community and mobilize effective modes of addressing these needs?

Are you overly involved in social needs? Do you overemphasize social concerns and drift towards a "social gospel"? Do you ride the hobby-horse or one particular point of view or one particular social policy issue? Do you tend to view people through the eyes of politics, economics or sociology rather than through the eyes of the God of the Bible?

Application Work Sheet

Part I. Personal Qualifications of Effective Ministers: Holiness

A. Humility

1. Do you acknowledge your limitations and needs out of confidence in Christ's gracious power?

2. Do you demonstrate a flexible spirit out of confidence in God's control over all things, God's authority over you, and God's presence with you?

B. Love

1. Do you have a positive approach to people because of confidence in the power and hope of the Gospel of Jesus Christ?

2. Do you show a servant's heart to people because you are first and foremost a servant of the Lord?

C. Integrity

1. Are you responsible to God first and foremost?

2. Do you demonstrate a disciplined lifestyle under the Lordship of Jesus?

3. Are your family commitments a proper priority under the Lord?

D. Spirituality

1. Do you demonstrate personal piety and vigor in your relationship with God?

2. Do you demonstrate faithfulness to the Bible and sound doctrine?

Part II: Functional Qualifications of Effective Ministers: Pastoral Skill

A. Nurture

1. Do you show involved caring that comes from genuine love in Christ for your brothers and sisters?

2. Do you counsel people the Lord's way?

3. Do you disciple others into maturity in Christ and use of their gifts?

4. Do you give yourself to discipline and to patrolling the boundaries of the church which God bought with His own blood?

B. Communication

1. Do you preach the whole counsel of God?

2. Do you provide education for God's many kinds of people?

3. Do you lead others to worship the Lord?

C. Leadership

1. Do you lead people into effective work together?

2. Do you administer well, creating a church that is wise in its stewardship?

3. Do you mediate fellowship among God's people?

4. Do you create cooperative and team ministry within the church and between churches that honor Christ?

D. Mission

1. Do you evangelize those outside of Jesus Christ?

2. Do you show social concern for the many needs of people whom God desires to address?

You have looked at yourself, hopefully through God's eyes. Now work with what you have seen.

If you could change in one area in the next year, which would it be? Where do you most need to mature in wisdom? What changes in you would bring the greatest glory to God and greatest blessing to other people?

Confess your sins and failings to God. Jesus Christ is your faithful high priest and shepherd. He is the Pastor of pastors. "Come with confidence to the throne of His grace that you may receive mercy and grace to help you in your time of need" (Hebrews 4:16). Believe it and do it. The Lord's strength is made perfect in your weakness.

Now what must you do? Prayerfully set goals. How will you become a more godly person and pastor? Are there people you must ask to pray for you and hold you accountable? Are there Bible passages or books you must study? Are there plans you must make? Do you need advice from a wise Christian about how to go about changing?

Appendix II
WHAT SHOULD A SERMON DO?

By Dr. William Hogan

FROM *RTS MINISTRY* (NOW BEING PUBLISHED AS *RTS REFORMED QUARTERLY*), VOLUME 11, NO. 1, SPRING 1991, P. 14. USED BY PERMISSION OF REFORMED THEOLOGICAL SEMINARY, JACKSON, ORLANDO, CHARLOTTE.

(Dr. Hogan was formerly the founder and senior pastor of the Church of the Savior in Wayne, Pennsylvania, and is currently Associate Professor of Preaching at Reformed Theological Seminary, Jackson, Mississippi.)

"Will this do?" asked a seminary student, anxiously awaiting the professor's evaluation of his sermon.

"Do what?" the professor replied, trying to make the student realize that every sermon must have some purpose. Scripture does not present truth in the abstract, but in applied form. In his famous Yale lectures on preaching, Henry Ward Beecher said, "A sermon is not like a Chinese firecracker to be fired off for the noise it makes. It is a hunter's gun, and at every discharge he should look to see his game fall."

What should a sermon do? Some books on preaching divide sermons into categories—those intended to inform, those intended to persuade or convince, or those intended to motivate. Ordinarily one of these three intentions will predominate, but to think that a sermon's aim is any one of them alone is inadequate. A sermon must address the whole person—mind, emotion and will.

A Sermon Should Make the Truth of Scripture Crystal Clear

First and foremost, a sermon must make the truth of Scripture crystal clear. Every Christian sermon must embody some significant biblical truth. Several years ago a well-known Christian magazine conducted a contest to discover the seminarian preacher of the year. Ironically, the winning sermon was almost totally devoid of distinctive Christian content, containing but one casual reference to Jesus. When a reader protested, the editor explained that, unfortunately, those who communicated well did not want to communicate the Gospel; those who did lacked good communication skills.

How tragic! Better a sermon that attempts to be faithful to the Word of God, but suffers from poor construction, than a piece of polished rhetoric with no biblical content. The truth revealed in God's written Word must be the essential substance of all preaching. Anything else is not Christian preaching!

To put it another way, all Christian preaching must be expository. The essence of exposition is, as the dictionary suggests, explanation. Expository preaching is rooted in the accurate explanation of Scripture and seeks to expose, or open up, some portion of the Bible.

The alternative to exposition is *imposition*, the travesty of imposing a foreign meaning upon a text. Scripture is not a piece of playdough to be molded into whatever shape the preacher desires. The preacher is always servant of the biblical text, not master of it. Stringing together a few blessed thoughts after skimming a portion of Scripture is inadequate for effective preaching. So is the "skyscraper" sermon—one story on top of another.

Any preacher who wants to please God and change his people through his pulpit work must be willing to devote time and effort to the study and interpretation of Scripture. And any church that wants solid preaching must be prepared to permit the pastor to have— indeed, to insist that he take—the time necessary for the task.

To be effective, the explanation must be clear. Some preaching is ineffective simply because it is confusing, and people aren't quite sure what the preacher is saying. Sometimes the lack of clarity begins in the preacher's mind; even *he* is not sure what he's trying to say. As Professor Howard Hendricks said: "A mist in the pulpit is a fog in the pew." Sometimes the difficulty lies in making the truth comprehensible to the ordinary listener, or, to quote Professor Hendricks again, in "putting the cookies on the lower shelf." If people are so amazed by the profundity or rhetorical eloquence of a sermon that they leave the service saying, "Wow! I would never in a million years have gotten *that* from that passage," then the preacher has failed. It is far better that they leave thinking, "Of course! Why didn't I see that? Now that he has explained it, the passage is plain."

A Sermon Should Stir the Heart

While accurate and clear explanation of biblical truth is fundamental, effective preaching requires something more. The truth must address the hearers not only on the cognitive level, but also on the affective, or feeling, level. Thus, *a sermon must help the listener feel the claim of the biblical text.* The truth revealed in Scripture is not given merely to be understood; that truth makes a claim upon our lives. It challenges our belief systems and our values. It demands change in our behavior. It is meant to remold our lives, from the inside out, from top to bottom. Effective preaching, therefore, must make the demand of the text both clear and compelling.

One of the most important factors in moving an audience emotionally is for them to see that the speaker himself is affected by what he is saying. Robert Dabney, in his classic book on preaching, *Sacred Rhetoric*, wrote, "If you would make others feel, you must feel yourself. . . . The heavenly flame must be kindled first in your own bosom, that by this law of sympathy it may radiate thence into the souls of your hearers." Dabney so valued this "principle of instinctive sympathy," that he called it the speaker's "right arm in the work of persuasion." However, he warned that the preacher's emotions must be genuine and not excessive. Nevertheless, the audience must recognize that what he says has gripped his heart if he expects it to grip theirs.

Furthermore, people will respond on an emotional level to preaching that touches some need in their lives. If they find the preacher's vocabulary is rich, his manner appealing, and his stories interesting, they may be entertained, but they are not likely to *do* anything with what they hear until they recognize its relevance to their lives.

While good preaching meets a congregation's felt needs, they should not set the agenda for the pulpit. The preacher who always tries to spot needs and search for texts to address them can hardly avoid unbalanced preaching. Usually, the more dysfunctional members of the congregation more openly express their needs. Consequently, the preacher who listens to the complaints of his congregation in order to decide the subject of next Sunday's sermon risks missing the needs of the less complaining, and probably more mature, members of the congregation. It's a matter of "the squeaky wheel getting the oil."

The better method is to preach consecutively through books or major sections of Scripture, seeking with each text to discern the need which precipitated the writing of that text in the first place, and then discerning where that same need arises today. The human condition has not changed, nor has God's solution. The problems with which we grapple today may present themselves in new shapes, but essentially they are the same issues with which men and women have always struggled.

Preaching which stimulates the imagination also helps Scriptural truth impact listeners. The preacher should not be content with merely telling people *about* the Bible; he must seek to *recreate* it, to bring it to life in this time, for these people. To know that Abraham struggled with faith is not enough; people must be led to take fresh steps in their own walks. To hear that Isaiah had an overpowering vision of God is not enough; a congregation must be overwhelmed themselves by the sovereign majesty and holiness of Jehovah. To learn about repentance is not enough; they must be led to repent.

Effective illustrations can also play an important part in stimulating the imagination. We often think of illustrations as devices used to clarify the truth, but that is only one of their functions, and probably not the most significant. More importantly, illustrations can stir the emotions. By telling how the truth under consideration worked in a specific instance, people can identify with the subject of the example and thus imagine what that same truth might be like in their own experience.

Similes and metaphors can also stimulate the imagination. For example, consider the matter of defining sin. The Westminster Shorter Catechism definition—*"any transgression of or want of conformity unto the law of God"*—is adequate as a theological construct, but it is aimed at the cognitive dimension, not the feeling level. Contrast that definition with the images Scripture used—being a sinner is like: becoming a prostitute when one is married, rebelling against a father's love and leaving home, wandering into danger like stupid sheep, being turned away from a party for not being properly dressed, being blind or crippled or deaf or diseased, outrunning a bear only to be bitten by a snake in the supposed safety of one's own home. These figures do more than help us understand what sin is. They help us feel something of its consequences.

A Sermon Should Press the Truth Upon the Will

A sermon not only must make the truth clear and help the listener feel its claim, but it also must *press that claim upon the hearer's will.*

For whatever reasons, some preachers seem reticent to appeal directly to the will of their hearers. Scripture, however, knows nothing of such reticence. In the Gospel, "God commands all men everywhere to repent" (Acts 17:30). The apostle Paul recognized that those who proclaim the Word of God are, in a real sense, the mouthpieces of God, so that when they preach the Word it is as though "God were entreating through us; we beg you on behalf of Christ, be reconciled to God" (II Corinthians 5:20). Preaching that is truly biblical, then, must appeal to the will. It must command, appeal, and plead, as the Apostles did. It must reprove, rebuke, and exhort, as Paul instructed Timothy to do (I Timothy 4:2).

A Sermon's Final Goal

The ultimate purpose of all preaching is to lead the listener to a whole-person encounter with the truth of God. His mind should understand the truth, his heart should be stirred to feel the claim of that truth, and his will should be moved to respond to that truth.

This whole-person encounter with the truth of God is, finally, the means to a further end—an encounter with the God of truth Himself. Preaching must enable listeners to hear the voice of God saying to them today what He said to the first listeners and to experience Him doing in them what He originally sought to do in the text. In short, the preacher should seek to make every sermon the occasion for listeners to have dealings with God.

Ultimately, of course, the effectiveness of preaching is the work of the Spirit. The most expertly crafted and powerfully delivered sermon imaginable will accomplish nothing if He does not act to persuade and enable the hearer to respond to the truth. But at the same time, we must also remember that the Spirit does not act in a vacuum. Ordinarily, He uses means, and preaching which employs all the rhetorical devices within the preacher's ability is one of those means.

When the Spirit in His sovereignty works with the Word in the heart of a listener, God's Word begins to change people. Attitudes, values, beliefs, and behavior are transformed, so that person either steps out of darkness into light, becoming a child of God and a citizen in His Kingdom, or, as a believer, moves another step along the path of sanctification. That, by God's grace, is what a sermon really ought to do.

BIBLIOGRAPHY

Personal Life

Adams, Jay E. *Shepherding God's Flock*. Grand Rapids, Mich.: Zondervan, 1986.

Alleine, Richard. *The World Conquered by the Faithful Christian*. Morgan, Penn.: Soli Deo Gloria, 1995 reprint.

Baxter, Richard. *The Reformed Pastor*. Edinburgh: Banner of Truth, 1979 reprint.

Bennett, Arthur, ed. *The Valley of Vision*. Edinburgh: Banner of Truth, 1975.

Bridges, Charles. *The Christian Ministry*. Edinburgh: Banner of Truth, 1967.

Bridges, Jerry. *The Pursuit of Holiness*. Colorado Springs: NavPress, 1978.

———. *The Practice of Godliness*. Colorado Springs: NavPress, 1983.

———. *Trusting God*. Colorado Springs: NavPress, 1988.

———. *The Joy of Fearing God*. Colorado Springs: Waterbrook, 1997.

Bunyan, John. *Pilgrim's Progress in Today's English*. Chicago: Moody, 1964.

———. "Prayer," in Vol. I, *Collected Works of John Bunyan*. Grand Rapids, Mich.: Baker, 1977. Also published separately by The Banner of Truth Trust, Edinburgh.

———. *The Holy War*. Chicago: Moody, 1948 reprint.

Calvin, John. *Golden Booklet of the True Christian Life*. Grand Rapids, Mich.: Baker, 1952.

Carson, D. A. *A Call to Spiritual Reformation*. Grand Rapids, Mich.: Baker, 1992.

———. *For the Love of God*. Wheaton, Ill.: Crossway Books, 1998.

Clowney, Edmund P. *Called to the Ministry.* Downers Grove, Ill.: InterVarsity, 1964.

————. *CM: Christian Meditation.* Nutley, N.J.: Craig Press, 1979.

Edwards, Jonathan. *Charity and Its Fruit.* Edinburgh: Banner of Truth, 1978.

————. *Religious Affections.* Sisters, Ore.: Multnomah, 1984 reprint.

Ferguson, Sinclair. *The Christian Life.* Edinburgh: Banner of Truth, 1981.

Flavel, John. *Keeping the Heart.* Morgan, Penn.: Soli Deo Gloria, 1998 reprint.

Getz, Gene A. *Praying for One Another.* Wheaton, Ill.: Victor Books, 1982.

Henry, Matthew. "Directions for Daily Communion With God," in Vol. I, *Complete Works of Matthew Henry.* Grand Rapids, Mich.: Baker, 1979.

Hughes, Kent. *Disciplines of a Godly Man.* Wheaton, Ill.: Crossway Books, 1991.

Kent, Homer A. *The Pastor and His Work.* Chicago: Moody, 1963.

Keller, W. Phillip. *A Shepherd Looks at Psalm 23.* Grand Rapids, Mich.: Eerdmans, 1987.

Law, William. *A Serious Call to a Devout and Holy Life.* Grand Rapids, Mich.: Eerdmans, 1966 reprint.

Lightfoot, Joseph Barber. *The Christian Ministry.* London: Macmillan, 1903.

Lloyd-Jones, D. Martyn. *Preaching and Preachers.* Grand Rapids, Mich.: Zondervan, 1971.

Lutzer, Erwin W. *Pastor to Pastor.* Grand Rapids, Mich.: Kregel, 1998.

MacArthur, John, Jr. *The Ultimate Priority.* Chicago: Moody, 1983.

————. *Drawing Near.* Wheaton, Ill.: Crossway Books, 1993.

————. *The Vanishing Conscience.* Dallas: Word, 1994.

————. *Rediscovering Pastoral Ministry.* Dallas: Word, 1995.

————. *Alone with God.* Wheaton, Ill.: Victor, 1995.

————. *The Pillars of Christian Character.* Wheaton, Ill.: Crossway Books, 1998.

Martin, Al. *What's Wrong With Preaching Today?* Edinburgh: Banner of Truth, n.d.

Murray, Andrew. *The Believer's Daily Renewal.* Minneapolis: Bethany House, 1981 reprint.

Murray, John. *Principles of Conduct.* Grand Rapids, Mich.: Eerdmans, 1957.

Packer, J. I. *Knowing God.* Downers Grove, Ill.: InterVarsity, 1973.

Peterson, Eugene C. *A Long Obedience in the Same Direction.* Downers Grove, Ill.: InterVarsity, 1980.

————. *Working the Angles: The Shape of Pastoral Integrity.* Grand Rapids, Mich.: Eerdmans, 1987.

Piper, John. *A Godward Life.* Sisters, Ore.: Multnomah, 1997.

————. *Desiring God.* Sisters, Ore.: Multnomah, 1986.

Prior, Kenneth. *The Way of Holiness.* Downers Grove, Ill.: InterVarsity, 1982.

Ryle, John Charles. *Practical Religion.* Cambridge: James Clark & Co., 1970 reprint.

————. *Holiness.* Durham, England: Evangelical Press, 1997 reprint.

Sanders, J. Oswald. *Spiritual Leadership.* Chicago: Moody, 1967.

Sherman, Doug and William Hendriksen. *Keeping Your Ethical Edge Sharp.* Colorado Springs: NavPress, 1990.

Spurgeon, C. H. *An All-Round Ministry.* Pasadena, TX: Pilgrim, 1973.

————. *Lectures to My Students.* Grand Rapids, Mich.: Baker, 1980.

————. *Morning and Evening.* Hendrickson, Mass.: Hendrickson Publishers, 1991 reprint.

Spring, Gardner. *The Distinguishing Traits of Christian Character.* Phillipsburg, N.J.: Presbyterian and Reformed, 1967.

Stedman, Ray C. *Talking to my Father: What Jesus Teaches About Prayer.* Sisters, Ore.: Multnomah, 1984.

Stott, John R. *The Preacher's Portrait*. Grand Rapids, Mich.: Eerdmans, 1964.

Thomas, W. H. Griffith. *Ministerial Life and Walk*. Grand Rapids, Mich.: Baker, 1974.

Tozer, A. W. *The Knowledge of the Holy*. New York: Harper, 1961.

————. *The Pursuit of God*. Camp Hill, Penn.: Christian Publications, 1987.

Weber, Stu. *Tender Warrior—God's Intention for a Man*. Sisters, Ore.: Multnomah, 1993.

Whitney, Donald S. *Spiritual Disciplines for the Christian Life*. Colorado Springs: NavPress, 1991.

Family Life

Adams, Jay E. *Christian Living in the Home*. Phillipsburg, N.J.: Presbyterian & Reformed, 1972.

Alexander, James W. *Thoughts on Family Worship*. Morgan, Penn.: Soli Deo Gloria, 1998 reprint.

Blackwood, Carolyn Phillips. *The Pastor's Wife*. Philadelphia: Westminster, 1951.

Brandt, Henry R. and Homer E. Dowdy. *Building a Christian Home*. Wheaton, Ill.: Scripture Press, 1960.

Campbell, Ross and Pat Likes. *How to Really Love Your Teenager*. Wheaton, Ill.: Victor, 1981.

————. *How to Really Know Your Child*. Wheaton, Ill.: Victor, 1987.

Cromarty, Jim. *A Book for Family Worship*. Durham, England: Evangelical Press, 1996.

Gangel, Kenneth Otto and Elisabeth Gangel. *Building a Christian Family*. Chicago: Moody, 1987.

Gangel, Kenneth Otto. *The Family First*. Minneapolis: His International Service, 1972.

Getz, Gene A. *The Measure of a Family*. Glendale, Calif.: Regal, 1976.

Hunt, Susan. *Spiritual Mothering*. Wheaton, Ill.: Crossway Books, 1992.

James, John Angell. *The Christian Father's Present to His Children*. Morgan, Penn.: Soli Deo Gloria, 1993 reprint.

————. *Female Piety*. Morgan, Penn.: Soli Deo Gloria, 1994 reprint.

————. *Addresses to Young Men*. Morgan, Penn.: Soli Deo Gloria, 1995 reprint.

————. *A Help to Domestic Happiness*. Morgan, Penn.: Soli Deo Gloria, 1995 reprint.

Kesler, Jay and Ronald A. Beers. *Parents & Teenagers*. Wheaton, Ill.: Victor, 1984.

Kistler, Don, ed. *The Godly Family*. Morgan, Penn.: Soli Deo Gloria, 1993.

LaHaye, Tim. *The Battle For the Family*. Chicago: Moody, 1993.

London, H. B., Jr. and Neil B. Wiseman. *Pastors at Risk*. Wheaton, Ill.: Victor, 1993.

Lepine, Bob. *The Christian Husband*. Ann Arbor, Mich.: Servant, 1999.

MacArthur, John, Jr. *The Family*. Chicago: Moody, 1982.

————. *Your Family*. Chicago: Moody, 1983.

————. *Successful Christian Parenting*. Nashville: Word, 1998.

Mack, Wayne. *Strengthening Your Marriage*. Phillipsburg, N.J.: Presbyterian & Reformed, 1977.

————. *Your Family—God's Way*. Phillipsburg, N.J.: Presbyterian & Reformed, 1991.

Mayhue, Richard. "The Pastor's Home" (Chapter 9), in John MacArthur, Jr. *Rediscovering Pastoral Ministry*. Dallas: Word, 1995.

Murray, Andrew. *How to Raise Your Children for Christ*. Minneapolis: Bethany House, 1975 reprint.

Ortlund, Anne. *Disciplines of the Beautiful Woman*. Waco: Word, 1977.

Peace, Martha. *Becoming a Titus 2 Woman.* Bemidji, Minn.: Focus, 1997.

————. *The Excellent Wife.* Bemidji, Minn.: Focus, n. d.

Piper, John and Wayne Grudem. *Recovering Biblical Manhood and Womanhood.* Wheaton, Ill.: Crossway Books, 1991.

Priola, Lou. *The Heart of Anger—Practical Help for the Prevention and Cure of Anger in Children.* Amityville, N. Y.: Calvary Press, 1997.

Rainey, Dennis. *Staying Close—Stopping the Natural Drift Toward Isolation In Marriage.* Dallas: Word, 1989.

Redd, Kate, Connie Neal, and Steve Woodworth. *Getting Your House (and Life) in Order.* New York: Galahad Books, 1994.

Small, Dwight. *Design for Christian Marriage.* Old Tappan, N.J.: Fleming H. Revell, 1959.

Stedman, Ray C., et al. *Family Life.* Waco: Word, 1976.

Tripp, Paul David. *Age of Opportunity—A Biblical Guide to Parenting Teens.* Phillipsburg, N.J.: Presbyterian & Reformed, 1997.

Tripp, Tedd. *Shepherding a Child's Heart.* Wapwallopen, Penn.: Shepherd Press, 1995.

Weber, Stu. *Tender Warrior—God's Intention for Man.* Sisters, Ore.: Multnomah, 1993.

Wheat, Ed. *Love Life for Every Married Couple.* Grand Rapids, Mich.: Zondervan, 1980.

Wheat, Ed and Gaye. *Intended for Pleasure.* Old Tappan, N.J.: Fleming H. Revell, 1977.

Zuck, Roy B. and Gene A. Getz, eds. *Ventures in Family Living.* Chicago: Moody, 1971.

Study Habits

Arthur, Kay. *How to Study Your Bible.* Eugene, Ore.: Harvest House, 1994.

Berkhof, L. *Principles of Biblical Interpretation.* Grand Rapids, Mich.: Baker, 1950.

Danker, Frederick W. *Multipurpose Tools for Bible Study*. Minneapolis: Fortress, 1993.

Kaiser, Walter C. *Toward an Exegetical Theology*. Grand Rapids, Mich.: Baker, 1981.

————— and Moises Silva. *An Introduction to Biblical Hermeneutics*. Grand Rapids, Mich.: Zondervan, 1994.

Kantzer, Kenneth S., ed. *Applying the Scriptures*. Grand Rapids, Mich.: Zondervan/Academie Books, 1987.

MacArthur, John, Jr. *How to Get the Most From God's Word*. Dallas: Word, 1997.

—————, ed. *Rediscovering Expository Preaching*. Dallas: Word, 1992.

See particularly these chapters:

Chapter 7: "Hermeneutics and Expository Preaching" by James E. Rosscup.

Chapter 8: "Exegesis and Expository Preaching" by Robert L. Thomas.

Chapter 9: "Grammatical Analysis and Expository Preaching" by George J. Zemek.

Chapter 10: "Study Tools for Expository Preaching" by James F. Stitzinger.

Chapter 11: "A Study Method for Expository Preaching" by John MacArthur, Jr.

Chapter 12: "The Pastor's Study" by John MacArthur, Jr. and Robert L. Thomas.

Maier, Gerhard. *Biblical Hermeneutics*. Wheaton, Ill.: Crossway Books, 1994.

McDowell, Josh. *Guide to Understanding Your Bible*. San Bernardino, Calif.: Here's Life, 1982.

Mickelsen, A. Berkeley. *Interpreting the Bible*. Grand Rapids, Mich.: Eerdmans, 1963.

Pink, A. W. *Profiting From the Word*. Edinburgh: Banner of Truth, 1970 reprint.

Ramm, Bernard L. *Protestant Biblical Interpretation*. Grand Rapids, Mich.: Baker, 1970.

————, et al. *Hermeneutics*. Grand Rapids, Mich.: Baker, 1967.

Sproul R. C. *Knowing Scripture*. Downers Grove, Ill.: InterVarsity, 1977.

Stott, James Robert Walmsey. *Understanding the Bible*. Grand Rapids, Mich.: Zondervan, 1979.

Warfield, Benjamin Breckenridge. *The Inspiration and Authority of the Bible*. Phillipsburg, N.J.: Presbyterian & Reformed, 1970 reprint.

*Discount and Direct Book and Tape Sellers
(Catalogs Available)*

Audubon Press, P.O. Box 8055, Laurel, MS 39441-8000.

Christian Book Distributors, P.O. Box 7000, Peabody, MA 01961-7000.

Cumberland Valley Bible Book Service, P.O. Box 613, 133 N. Hanover St., Carlisle, PA 17013.

Desiring God Ministries, 720 13th Avenue South, Minneapolis, MN 55415-1793.

E4 Group, P.O. Box 1505, Escondido, CA 92033.

Kregel Publications (and Kregel Used Books), P.O. Box 2607, Grand Rapids, MI 49501-2607.

Naphtali Press, P.O. Box 141084, Dallas, TX 75214.

Presbyterian & Reformed Direct, P.O. Box 109, Phillipsburg, NJ 08865.

Reformation & Revival, P.O. Box 88216, Carol Stream, IL 60188.

Reformation Heritage Books, 2919 Leonard NE, Grand Rapids, MI 49505.

Reformation Resources (Alliance of Confessing Evangelicals), P.O. Box 2000, Philadelphia, PA 19103-8440.

Soli Deo Gloria, P.O. Box 451, Morgan, PA 15064.

Spring Arbor Distributors, 10885 Textile Rd., Belleville, MI 48111-2398.

Still Waters Revival Books, 4710-37A Avenue, Edmonton, AB Canada T6L 375.

Tabernacle Bookshop, Metropolitan Tabernacle, Elephant & Castle, London, SE1 6SD, England.

The Banner of Truth Trust (USA Office), P.O. Box 621, Carlisle, PA 17013.

Special Internet Booksellers

Amazon.com: Hardcover books at 30% discount; paperback 20%; virtually any book in print; will search for rare and out-of-print books. Web address: www.amazon.com

Buybooks.com: Hardcover books at 40% discount; guaranteed 10% below online competitors. Web address: www.buybooks.com

Messages

Adams, Jay E. *Pulpit Speech*. Phillipsburg: N.J.: Presbyterian & Reformed, 1971.

————. *Preaching with Purpose*. Phillipsburg, N.J.: Presbyterian & Reformed, 1982.

Alexander, James W. *Thoughts on Preaching*. Carlisle, Penn.: Banner of Truth, 1975.

Bickel, R. Bruce. *Light and Heat: The Puritan View of the Pulpit*. Morgan, Penn.: Soli Deo Gloria, 1999 reprint.

Blackwood, Andrew Watterson. *Biographical Preaching for Today*. New York: Abingdon, 1953.

Broadus, John A. *On the Preparation and Delivery of Sermons*. San Francisco: Harper & Row, 1979.

Carson, D. A. *Exegetical Fallacies*. Grand Rapids, Mich.: Baker, 1984.

————. *King James Version Debate*. Grand Rapids, Mich.: Baker, 1979.

Chapell, Bryan. *Christ-Centered Preaching*. Grand Rapids, Mich.: Baker, 1994.

————. *Using Illustrations to Preach With Power*. Grand Rapids, Mich.: Zondervan, 1992.

Clowney, Edmund P. *Preaching and Biblical Theology*. Grand Rapids, Mich.: Eerdmans, 1961.

Eby, David. *Power Preaching for Church Growth—The Role of Preaching in Growing Churches*. Ross-shire, England: Christian Focus, 1996.

Hendricks, Howard. *Teaching to Change Lives*. Sisters, Ore.: Multnomah, 1987.

Kaiser, Walter C. *Towards An Exegetical Theology—Biblical Exegesis for Preaching and Teaching*. Grand Rapids, Mich.: Baker, 1981.

Kubo, Sakae and Walter Sprecht. *So Many Versions*. Grand Rapids, Mich.: Zondervan, 1975.

Larsen, David L. *The Anatomy of Preaching*. Grand Rapids, Mich.: Baker, 1989.

Lloyd-Jones, D. Martyn. *Preaching and Preachers*. Grand Rapids, Mich.: Zondervan, 1972.

Logan, Samuel T., Jr. *The Preacher and Preaching*. Phillipsburg, N.J.: Presbyterian and Reformed, 1986.

Martin, Robert. *Accuracy of Translation*. Edinburgh: Banner of Truth, 1989.

MacArthur, John, Jr. *Rediscovering Expository Preaching*. Dallas: Word, 1992.

McDill, Wayne. *The 12 Essential Skills for Great Preaching*. Nashville: Broadman & Holman, 1994.

Olford, Stephen F. *Anointed Expository Preaching*. Nashville: Broadman & Holman, 1996.

Piper, John. *The Supremacy of God in Preaching*. Grand Rapids, Mich.: Baker, 1990.

Robinson, Haddon W. *Biblical Preaching: The Development and Delivery of Expository Messages*. Grand Rapids, Mich.: Baker, 1980.

Sire, James. *Scripture Twisting*. Downers Grove, Ill.: InterVarsity, 1980.

Spurgeon, C. H. *Lectures to My Students*. Grand Rapids, Mich.: Baker, 1980 reprint.

Stalker, James. *The Preacher and His Models*. Grand Rapids, Mich.: Baker, 1967.

Stott, John R. W. *The Preacher's Portrait.* Grand Rapids, Mich.: Eerdmans, 1961.

———. *Between Two Worlds.* Grand Rapids, Mich.: Eerdmans, 1982.

Vines, Jerry A. *A Practical Guide to Sermon Preparation.* Chicago: Moody, 1985.

———. *A Guide to Effective Sermon Delivery.* Chicago: Moody Press, 1986.

White, James. *King James Only Controversy.* Minneapolis: Bethany House, 1995.

Wiersbe, Warren W. *Preaching and Teaching with Imagination.* Wheaton, Ill.: Victor, 1974.

Woods, Arthur Skevington. *The Art of Preaching: Message, Method and Motive in Preaching.* Grand Rapids, Mich.: Zondervan, 1964.

Zuck, Roy B. *Teaching with Spiritual Power.* Grand Rapids, Mich.: Kregel, 1993.

———. *Teaching as Jesus Taught.* Grand Rapids, Mich.: Baker, 1995.

———. *Teaching as Paul Taught.* Grand Rapids, Mich.: Baker, 1998.

———. *Spirit-Filled Preaching.* Nashville: Word, 1998.

Church Life

Adams, Jay E. *Shepherding God's Flock.* Grand Rapids, Mich.: Zondervan, 1974.

———. *Ready to Restore.* Phillipsburg, N.J.: Presbyterian and Reformed, 1981.

———. *Handbook of Church Discipline.* Grand Rapids, Mich.: Zondervan, 1986.

Anderson, Robert C. *The Effective Pastor.* Chicago: Moody, 1985.

Augustine. *City of God.* New York: E.P. Dutton, 1956 reprint.

Baxter, Richard. *The Reformed Pastor.* Edinburgh: Banner of Truth, 1979 reprint.

Berghoef, Gerard and Lester De Koster. *Elders Handbook*. Grand Rapids, Mich.: Christian Library Press, 1979.

Betters, Sharon W. *Treasures of Encouragement—Women Helping Women in the Church*. Phillipsburg, N.J.: Presbyterian and Reformed, 1996.

Blackwood, Andrew Watterson. *Pastoral Work*. Grand Rapids, Mich.: Baker, 1944.

Bridges, Charles. *The Christian Ministry*. Edinburgh: Banner of Truth, 1980 reprint.

Bridges, Jerry. *The Crisis of Caring—Recovering the Meaning of True Fellowship*. Phillipsburg, N.J.: Presbyterian and Reformed, 1987.

Bromiley, G. W. *Christian Ministry*. Grand Rapids, Mich.: Eerdmans, 1959.

Buzzard, Lynn R. and Lawrence Eck. *Tell It to the Church— Reconciling out of Court*. Elgin, Ill.: David C. Cook, 1982.

Chapell, Bryan. *The 21st Century Pastor*. Grand Rapids, Mich.: Baker, 1994.

Clowney, Edmund P. *The Biblical Doctrine of the Church*. Philadelphia: Westminster Theological Seminary, 1979.

Conn, Harvey M. *Practical Theology and the Ministry of the Church*. Phillipsburg, N.J.: Presbyterian and Reformed, 1990.

Dale, Robert D. *Surviving Difficult Church Members*. Nashville: Abingdon, 1984.

————. *Pastoral Leadership*. Nashville: Abingdon, 1986.

Dickson, David. *The Elder & His Work*. Dallas: Presbyterian Heritage, 1990.

Eyres, Lawrence R. *The Elders of the Church*. Phillipsburg, N.J.: Presbyterian and Reformed, 1975.

Frame, John M. *Evangelical Reunion: Denominations and the Body of Christ*. Grand Rapids, Mich.: Baker, 1991.

Getz, Gene A. *Sharpening the Focus of the Church*. Chicago: Moody, 1974.

————. *Building up One Another*. Wheaton, Ill.: Victor, 1986.

Hughes, Kent and Barbara. *Liberating Ministry from the Success Syndrome*. Wheaton, Ill.: Tyndale, 1987.

Hull, Bill. *Can We Save the Evangelical Church?* Grand Rapids, Mich.: Baker, 1993.

Hurley, James B. *Man and Woman in Biblical Perspective*. Grand Rapids, Mich.: Zondervan/Academie Books, 1981.

Jeschke, Marlin. *Discipling the Brother*. Scottsdale, Penn.: Herald Press, 1972.

Jefferson, Charles. *The Building of the Church*. Grand Rapids, Mich.: Baker, 1969.

————. *The Minister As Shepherd*. Hong Kong: Living Books, 1973.

Keller, Timothy J. *Ministries of Mercy*. Phillipsburg, N.J.: Presbyterian and Reformed, 1997.

Kent, Homer A. *The Pastor and His Work*. Chicago: Moody, 1963.

Kostenberger, Andreas J., Thomas R. Schreiner, and H. Scott Baldwin, eds. *Women in the Church*. Grand Rapids, Mich.: Baker, 1995.

Kuiper, Rienk Bouke. *The Glorious Body of Christ*. Grand Rapids, Mich.: Eerdmans, 1955.

Laney, J. Carl. *A Guide to Church Discipline*. Minneapolis: Bethany House, 1985.

London, H. B., Jr. and Neil B. Wiseman. *Pastors at Risk*. Wheaton, Ill.: Victor, 1993.

MacArthur, John, Jr. *Shepherdology*. Panorama City, Calif.: The Master's Fellowship, 1989.

————. *The Master's Plan for the Church*. Chicago: Moody, 1991.

————. *Ashamed of the Gospel: When the Church Becomes Like the World*. Wheaton, Ill.: Crossway Books, 1993.

————. *The Body Dynamic*. Colorado Springs: Chariot/Victor, 1996.

Mack, Wayne A. and David Swavely. *The Role of Women in the Church*. Cherry Hill, N.J.: Mack Publishing, 1972.

————. *Life in the Father's House—A Member's Guide to the*

Local Church. Phillipsburg, N.J.: Presbyterian and Reformed, 1996.

Means, James E. *Effective Pastors for a New Century.* Grand Rapids, Mich.: Baker, 1993.

Murray, Thomas. *Pastoral Theology—The Pastor in the Various Duties of His Office.* Audubon, N.J.: Old Paths Publications, 1996 reprint.

Robertson, A. T. *The Glory of the Ministry.* Grand Rapids, Mich.: Baker, 1979.

Ryrie, Charles Caldwell. *The Place of Women in the Church.* Chicago: Moody, 1958.

Salter, Darius. *What Really Matters in Ministry.* Grand Rapids, Mich.: Baker, 1990.

Sanders, Oswald. *Spiritual Leadership.* Chicago: Moody, 1980.

Spurgeon, C. H. *Lectures to My Students.* Grand Rapids, Mich.: Baker, 1977 reprint.

————. *An All-Round Ministry.* Pasadena, Tex..: Pilgrim, 1983 reprint.

Stalker, James. *The Preacher and His Models.* Grand Rapids, Mich.: Baker, 1967.

Stott, John. *The Preacher's Portrait.* Grand Rapids, Mich.: Eerdmans, 1961.

Strauch, Alexander. *Biblical Eldership: An Urgent Call to Restore Biblical Church Leadership.* Littleton, Colo.: Lewis and Roth, 1988.

————. *The New Testament Deacon.* Littleton, Colo.: Lewis and Roth, 1992.

Sugden, Howard F. and Warren W. Wiersbe. *Confident Pastoral Leadership.* Grand Rapids, Mich.: Baker, 1993.

Thomas, W. H. Griffith. *Ministerial Life and Walk.* Grand Rapids, Mich.: Baker, 1974 reprint.

Wagner, Charles U. *The Pastor—His Life and Work.* Schaumburg, Ill.: Regular Baptist Press, 1976.

Walker, Warham. *Harmony in the Church—Church Discipline.* Rochester, N.Y.: Backus Books, 1981 reprint.

Whitney, Donald W. *Spiritual Disciplines Within the Church.* Chicago: Moody, 1996.

Wiersbe, Warren W. and David Wiersbe. *Making Sense of the Ministry.* Grand Rapids, Mich.: Baker, 1989.

Wright, Eric. *Church—No Spectator Sport.* Durham, England: Evangelical Press, 1994.

Counseling

(For brevity, only a few of Jay Adams's approximately seventy-five books and pamphlets will be listed below. However, each one of his works is strongly recommended.)

Adams, Jay E. *Competent to Counsel.* Grand Rapids, Mich.: Zondervan, 1970.

————. *The Big Umbrella and Other Essays and Addresses on Christian Counseling.* Phillipsburg, N.J.: Presbyterian and Reformed, 1972.

————. *Godliness Through Discipline* Phillipsburg, N.J.: Presbyterian and Reformed, 1972.

————. *The Christian Counselor's Manual.* Grand Rapids, Mich.: Zondervan, 1973.

————. *The Christian Counselor's Casebook.* Grand Rapids, Mich.: Zondervan, 1974.

————. *Lectures on Counseling.* Grand Rapids, Mich.: Zondervan, 1975.

————. *The Use of Scriptures in Counseling.* Phillipsburg, N.J.: Presbyterian and Reformed, 1975.

————. *What About Nouthetic Counseling?* Grand Rapids, Mich.: Baker, 1976.

————. *The Christian Counselor's New Testament: A New Translation in Everyday English with Notations, Marginal References, and Supplemental Helps.* Phillipsburg, N.J.: Presbyterian and Reformed, 1977.

————. *Helps for Counseling.* Grand Rapids, Mich.: Baker, 1977.

————. *A Theology of Christian Counseling.* Grand Rapids, Mich.: Zondervan, 1979.

————. *The Christian Counselor's Workbook*. Phillipsburg, N.J.: Presbyterian and Reformed, 1981.

————. *The Language of Counseling*. Phillipsburg, N.J.: Presbyterian and Reformed, 1981.

————. *Ready to Restore: The Layman's Guide to Christian Counseling*. Phillipsburg, N.J.: Presbyterian and Reformed, 1981.

————. *The Biblical View of Self-Esteem, Self-Love, Self-Image*. Eugene, Ore.: Harvest House, 1986.

————. *Handbook of Church Discipline*. Grand Rapids, Mich.: Zondervan, 1986.

————. *How to Help People Change: The Four-Step Biblical Process*. Grand Rapids, Mich.: Zondervan, 1986.

————. *Winning The War Within—A Biblical Strategy for Spiritual Warfare*. Woodruff, S.C.: Timeless Texts, 1996.

————. *Counsel from Psalm 119*. Woodruff, S.C.: Timeless Texts, 1998.

Bobgan, Martin, and Deidre Bobgan. *Hypnosis and the Christian*. Minneapolis: Bethany, 1984.

————. *How to Counsel from Scripture*. Chicago: Moody, 1985). (The Bobgans have other works, too numerous to mention, that can also be helpful.)

Brownback, Paul. *The Danger of Self Love*. Chicago: Moody, 1982.

Buckley, Ed. *Why Christians Can't Trust Psychology*. Eugene, Ore.: Harvest House, 1994.

Colquhoun, John. *Spiritual Comfort*. Morgan, Penn.: Soli Deo Gloria, 1998 reprint.

Eyrich, Howard A. *Three to Get Ready: A Christian Premarital Counselor's Manual*. Phillipsburg, N.J.: Presbyterian and Reformed, 1978.

Hindson, Ed and Howard Eyrich. *Totally Sufficient*. Eugene, Ore.: Harvest House, 1997.

Kruis, John G. *Quick Scripture Reference for Counseling*. Grand Rapids, Mich.: Baker, 1988.

Lloyd-Jones, D. Martyn. *Spiritual Depression: Its Causes and Cure.* Grand Rapids, Mich.: Eerdmans, 1965.

MacArthur, John, Jr. and Wayne Mack, eds. *Our Sufficiency in Christ.* Dallas: Word, 1991; repr. Wheaton, Ill.: Crossway, 1998.

—————. *Introduction to Biblical Counseling.* Dallas: Word, 1994.

Playfair, William L. *The Useful Lie.* Wheaton, Ill.: Crossway Books, 1991.

Sande, Ken. *The Peacemaker: A Biblical Guide to Resolving Personal Conflict.* Grand Rapids, Mich.: Baker, 1990.

Symonds, Joseph. *The Case and Cure of a Deserted Soul.* Morgan, Penn.: Soli Deo Gloria, 1996 reprint.

Watson, Thomas. *The Art of Divine Contentment.* Morgan, Penn.: Soli Deo Gloria, reprint from 1835 edition.

Welch, Edward T. *Counselor's Guide to the Brain and Its Disorders: Knowing the Difference Between Disease and Sin.* Grand Rapids, Mich.: Zondervan, 1991.

Whitney, Donald S. *Spiritual Disciplines for the Christian Life.* Colorado Springs: NavPress, 1991.

Weddings, Divorces, Funerals

Adams, Jay E. *Christian Living in the Home.* Phillipsburg, N.J.: Presbyterian and Reformed, 1972.

—————. *Marriage, Divorce, and Remarriage in the Bible.* Grand Rapids, Mich.: Zondervan, 1980.

Blackburn, William. *What You Should Know About Suicide.* Dallas: Word, 1982.

Coleman, William L. *Understanding Suicide.* Elgin, Ill.: David C. Cook, 1979.

Eyrich, Howard A. *Three to Get Ready: A Christian Premarital Counselor's Manual.* Phillipsburg, N.J.: Presbyterian and Reformed, 1978.

Goulooze, William. *The Christian Worker's Handbook.* Grand Rapids, Mich.: Baker, 1953.

Hart, Archibald D. *Children and Divorce: What to Expect, How to Help*. Dallas: Word, 1982.

House, H. Wayne, ed. *Divorce and Remarriage—Four Christian Views*. Downers Grove, Ill.: InterVarsity, 1990.

Hurley, James B. *Man and Woman in Biblical Perspective*. Grand Rapids, Mich.: Zondervan/Academie Books, 1981.

Irion, Paul E. *The Funeral and the Mourners: Pastoral Care of the Bereaved*. Nashville: Abingdon, 1979.

James, John Angell. *The Widow Directed to the Widow's God*. Morgan, Penn.: Soli Deo Gloria, 1996 reprint.

Lutzer, Erwin W. *Matters of Life and Death*. Chicago: Moody, 1994.

Mack, Wayne A. *Strengthening Your Marriage*. Phillipsburg, N.J.: Presbyterian and Reformed, 1977.

————. *Your Family God's Way: Developing and Sustaining Relationships in the Home*. Phillipsburg, N.J.: Presbyterian and Reformed, 1991.

Murray, John. *Divorce*. Grand Rapids, Mich.: Baker, 1961.

Piper, John and Wayne Grudem, eds. *Recovering Biblical Manhood and Womanhood: A Response to Evangelical Feminism*. Wheaton, Ill.: Crossway Books, 1990.

Stott, John R. W. *Divorce*. Downers Grove, Ill.: InterVarsity, 1973.

Wiersbe, Warren Wendell and David W. Wiersbe. *Comforting the Bereaved*. Chicago: Moody, 1985.

Relationships With Others

Aldrich, Joseph C. *Life-Style Evangelism: Crossing Traditional Boundaries to Reach the Unbelieving World*. Sisters, Ore.: Multnomah, 1981.

Blanchard, John. *Right With God*. Carlisle, Penn.: Banner of Truth, 1971.

————. *Ultimate Questions*. Darlington, England: Evangelical Press, 1987.

Bonar, Horatius. *Words to Winners of Souls*. New York: American Tract Society, 1950 reprint.

Borchert, Gerald L. *Dynamics of Evangelism*. Dallas: Word, 1976.

Bruce, A. B. *Training of the Twelve*. Grand Rapids, Mich.: Zondervan, 1963.

Dayton, Edward R. and David Allen Fraser. *Planning Strategies for World Evangelization*. Grand Rapids, Mich.: Eerdmans, 1980.

Elliot, James. *The Journal of Jim Elliott*, ed. Elisabeth Elliott. Old Tappan, N.J.: Fleming H. Revell, 1978.

Gerstner, John H. *Jonathan Edwards, Evangelist*. Morgan, Penn.: Soli Deo Gloria, 1995 reprint.

Greenway, Roger S. *The Pastor-Evangelist*. Phillipsburg, N.J.: Presbyterian and Reformed, 1987.

Jeffers, Peter. *How Shall They Hear?* Durham, England: Evangelical Press, 1996.

Kuiper, R. B. *God Centered Evangelism*. Edinburgh: Banner of Truth, 1961.

Lewis, C. S. *Mere Christianity*. New York: Collier Books, 1943.

Little, Paul E. *How to Give Away Your Faith*. Downers Grove, Ill.: InterVarsity, 1966.

MacArthur, John, Jr. *Ashamed of the Gospel*. Wheaton, Ill.: Crossway Books, 1993.

—————. *The Gospel According to Jesus*. Grand Rapids, Mich.: Zondervan, 1994.

McCloskey, Mark. *Tell It Often—Tell It Well*. San Bernardino, Calif.: Here's Life, 1985.

Metzger, Will. *Tell the Truth: The Whole Gospel to the Whole Person by Whole People*. Downers Grove, Ill.: InterVarsity, 1981.

Murray, Andrew. *Key to the Missionary Problem*. Fort Washington, Penn.: Christian Literature Crusade, 1979 reprint.

Packer, J. I. *Evangelism and the Sovereignty of God*. Downers Grove, Ill.: InterVarsity, 1961.

Piper, John. *Let the Nations be Glad*. Grand Rapids, Mich.: Baker, 1993.

Pippert, Rebecca M. *Out of the Saltshaker and into the World*

(Evangelism as a Way of Life). Downers Grove, Ill.: InterVarsity, 1979.

Posterski, Donald C. *Reinventing Evangelism*. Downers Grove, Ill.: InterVarsity, 1989.

Reisinger, Ernest C. *Today's Evangelism: Its Message and Methods*. Phillipsburg, N.J.: Craig Press, 1982.

Stott, John R. W. *Our Guilty Silence: The Church, the Gospel, and the World*. Grand Rapids, Mich.: Eerdmans, 1969.

Watson, David. *I Believe in Evangelism*. Grand Rapids, Mich.: Eerdmans, 1977.

Wells, David F. *God the Evangelist*. Grand Rapids, Mich.: Eerdmans, 1987.

Wood, Arthur S. *Evangelism: Its Theology and Practice*. Grand Rapids, Mich.: Zondervan, 1966.

Dangers

Covey, Stephen R. *The 7 Habits of Highly Effective People*. New York: Simon & Schuster, 1989.

Engstrom, Theodore Wilhelm and Alex Mackenzie. *Managing Your Time*. Grand Rapids, Mich.: Zondervan, 1968.

Hummel, Charles E. *Freedom from the Tyranny of the Urgent*. Downers Grove, Ill.: InterVarsity, 1977.

Pastoral Temptations and Sins

Armstrong, John H. *Can Fallen Pastors Be Restored?* Chicago: Moody, 1995.

Bridges, Jerry. *Trusting God Even When Life Hurts*. Colorado Springs: NavPress, 1988.

Carson, D. A. *Exegetical Fallacies*. Grand Rapids, Mich.: Baker, 1984.

Foxe, John. *Foxe's Book of Martyrs*. Springdale, Penn.: Whitaker House, 1981 reprint.

Grenz, Stanley J. and Roy D. Bell. *Betrayal of Trust—Sexual Misconduct in the Pastorate*. Downers Grove, Ill.: InterVarsity, 1995.

Johnson, David and Jeff VanVonderon. *The Subtle Power of Spiritual Abuse.* Minneapolis: Bethany House, 1991.

Keller, W. Phillip. *Predators in Our Pulpits.* Eugene, Ore.: Harvest House, 1988.

LaHaye, Tim. *If Ministers Fall, Can They Be Restored?* Grand Rapids, Mich.: Zondervan, 1990.

London, H. B., Jr. and Neil B. Wiseman. *Pastors at Risk.* Wheaton, Ill.: Victor, 1993.

Murray, John. *Behind a Frowning Providence.* Edinburgh: Banner of Truth, 1990.

Rassieur, Charles. *The Problems Clergymen Don't Talk About.* Philadelphia: Westminster, 1976.

Sedgwick, Obadiah. *The Anatomy of Secret Sins.* Morgan, Penn.: Soli Deo Gloria, 1995 reprint.

Sire, James. *Scripture Twisting.* Downers Grove, Ill.: InterVarsity, 1980.

Vos, Johannes. *The Separated Life.* Philadelphia: Great Commission Publications, n.d.

Winebrenner, Jan and Debra Frazier. *When a Leader Falls.* Minneapolis: Bethany House, 1993.

Miscellaneous

Anderson, Robert C. *The Effective Pastor.* Chicago: Moody, 1985.

Armstrong, John H., ed. *The Compromised Church.* Wheaton, Ill.: Crossway Books, 1998.

Brekko, Milo L., Merton P. Strommen, and Dorothy L. Williams. *Ten Faces of Ministry.* Minneapolis: Augsburg, 1979.

Conn, Harvey M. *Practical Theology and the Ministry of the Church.* Phillipsburg: N.J.: Presbyterian and Reformed, 1990.

Hiltner, Seward. *The Christian Shepherd.* Nashville: Abingdon, 1980.

Killinger, John. *The Tender Shepherd.* Nashville: Abingdon, 1984.

Longnecker, Harold. *The Village Church: Its Pastor and Program.* Chicago: Moody, 1961.

Lutzer, Erwin. *Pastor to Pastor—Tackling the Problems of Ministry.* Grand Rapids, Mich.: Kregel, 1998.

Means, James. E. *Effective Pastors for a New Century.* Grand Rapids, Mich.: Baker, 1993.

Paul, Cecil R. *Passages of a Pastor.* Grand Rapids, Mich.: Zondervan, 1981.

Salter, Darius. *What Really Matters in Ministry.* Grand Rapids, Mich.: Baker, 1990.

Shelley, Marshall. *Well-Intentioned Dragons—Ministering to Problem People in the Church.* Minneapolis: Bethany House, 1985.

Stevens, R. Paul. *The Equipping Guide to Every-member Ministry.* Downers Grove, Ill.: InterVarsity, 1992.

Sugden, Howard F. and Warren W. Wiersbe. *Confident Pastoral Leadership—Practical Solutions to Perplexing Problems.* Chicago: Moody, 1973.

Sweet, Herman J. *The Multiple Staff in the Local Church.* Philadelphia: Westminster, 1963.

Thomas, W. H. Griffith. *Ministerial Life and Walk.* Grand Rapids, Mich.: Baker, 1974 reprint.

Westing, Harold J. *Multiple Church Staff Handbook.* Grand Rapids, Mich.: Kregel, 1985.

INDEX